Teacher Black. ...

By James Prescott-Kerr

Edited by Danielle Larkin

Cover by Jisu Pang

Copyright © 2021 James Prescott-Kerr

All rights reserved. No part of this publication may be reproduced, distributed, or transmitted in any form or by any means, including photocopying, recording, or other electronic or mechanical methods, without the prior written permission of the publisher, except in the case of brief quotations embodied in critical reviews and certain other noncommercial uses permitted by copyright law. For permission requests, email j.p-k@hotmail.com

Contents

Preface - Why China? (4)

Teacher's Training (22)

Welcome to Changzhou (61)

Weekend in Shanghai (81)

Being Big and Black in China (93)

The Swing of Things (104)

Golden Week (122)

Back to English (135)

Real Friends (144)

Happy Fake Birthday (150)

Rainy Days, Thanksgiving and Shanghai (161)

December (166)

25/12/2015 (176)

Happy New Year! (194)

Teacher Black (203)

Pre-Spring (214)

Macau And Hong Kong (222)

Halftime (233)

Back into The Swing of Things (241)

Setback (245)

Grieving Abroad (249)

Life Goes On (258)

Where's Your Passport? (264)

China Are Number 1! (272)

Good Times (278)

Football in China (284)

Humanitarian Hitler? (292)

Smile for The Camera (301)

Shanghai Goodbyes and Euro 16 (306)

Warming Down (312)

Farewell Changzhou, Teacher Black No More! (315)

Fin (326)

Post-China (340)

Preface – Why China?

I think it would be pointless for me to write a whole book about my life in China without giving some context beforehand. So, before I delve into the details of what was the most eventful year of my life, I will attempt to illustrate the scenery surrounding the roads leading to me boarding my flight to Beijing Capital International Airport.

The straightforward truth is I stumbled across an online advert whilst absent-mindedly trawling through vacancies, applied for a job via an agency, and got it. I saw the agency "Teach English In China" online and thought I'd enquire more via email once the website enticed me. I exchanged dialogue with the company's founder, Arnold, and secured myself an interview the following day. He called me at the arranged time, and as well as having a CV that suited the role, we hit it off pretty organically on a personal level. I felt more like I was talking to a friend as opposed to having an interview, and in hindsight, I was. We are still friends to this day. We meet up for drinks occasionally, and I am usually a guest speaker at his China networking events, giving personal and professional insight to potential teachers to what they'd experience professionally and culturally. To my delight, I'd passed the interview and was scheduled for the TEFL training course in Beijing.

Along with the technical process of how I got the role, I want to uncover a bit more detail on the seeds planted in my imagination that made the advert even spark the smallest interest on my part.

In recent years, preceding my adventure, I had developed a yearning to travel. Not just stopping off at different countries, staying in luxury resorts and hotels while soaking up sun rays at tourist attractions. I mean embracing the everyday culture and becoming a resident. I mean knocking elbows with people while eating the same food they were raised on and fed their children with, sharing stories over beers about working life, and exchanging opinions on local issues. These were the prospective experiences that started to excite me. I wanted to grow.

I was lucky enough to experience these things on my trip to South Africa in 2013. I was there for three weeks after flying over the day after my graduation. Dr. Gary Armstrong, one of my lecturers at Brunel University, recommended me to represent the Arsenal F.C. Community Coaching Scheme on their Gap Year programme. He was vocal about being impressed with my level of contributions in lectures and my quality of work submissions. After a successful coaching trial and interview, I was selected, and it ended up being a life-changing experience for me. The two coaches I went to South Africa with had the same feelings as I did. They were Jonny, who was already a coach for one of Arsenal's Youth Development teams, and Christine, whom I graduated alongside at Brunel, was also selected by Gary.

Despite us knowing of each other and being in many of the same lectures, Christine and I had never spoken until we were teamed up for this trip. We got on swimmingly, and Jonny completed what was a thoroughly enjoyable trio to be a part of. As well as all having a mutual love for football, our personalities also bounced off each other, and despite being in each other's company 24/7 for three weeks (Well, Christine had the luxury of her own bed in the evenings while Jonny and I got cosy in a double bed) we never shared either a dull or a remotely frustrating moment.

My perspective transformed far beyond what I could have expected in a three-week stint. Being in the Motherland for the first time also added to the homely feeling as I was surrounded by people who looked like me. I saw those who shared my skin tone on billboards and posters everywhere. It gave me a sense of belonging I had never felt before.

I spent my time there visiting communities all over Johannesburg and Pretoria, connecting with them through coaching and playing the game I loved more than anything. A new culture engulfed me, and the locals took me under their wing and encouraged me to make it my own. I was treated like family. Warmth radiated from them and flowed through me. I still have a deep fondness for South Africa and the friends I made over there. I stay updated with most of them via social media, and I have every intention of returning whenever my schedule and finances deem it as viable. It was a transformative experience for all three of us, and we even spoke about potentially returning to South Africa to once again work with Youth Zones, the Sporting Initiative that partnered with the Arsenal Community Scheme and felt more like family to us than hosts.

Hopefully, one day that still happens. Jonny moved stateside to further his coaching career. I still plan on visiting him there. He has been nice enough to offer a roof over my head, and it would be great catching up with him again. Christine has since moved to Australia and is now married. I almost felt like I would be letting the team down if I did not at least try to follow suit and add to my adventures abroad sooner or later. My experiences there opened my mind up to how much the world has to offer. The different climates I have yet to feel. Cultures I have yet to learn about, stories I have yet to hear, foods I have yet to eat, people I have yet to meet. I just knew this couldn't be the last time I ventured abroad, and the next time I did, I would want to stay for considerably longer.

I could have ended up in the US as well. In the Summer of 2014, I had signed up for an FA Level 2 football coaching course. I knew the step up from my Level 1 would qualify me to coach football in more places and at a higher level overseas. I was going to use my qualification as my ticket around the world. Coaching had already gotten me to South Africa, so why stop there? I had one eye on the USA because I knew Jonny was there and would help me with anything I needed. I had also spoken to a youth coach at LA Galaxy whom I knew from school.

He'd even offered to use his connections to help me find my feet once I had built up a strong enough CV. So, in terms of desirability and my network, either LA or New York, seemed an eventual certainty.

I stumbled across the opportunity to gain another qualification to expand on my credentials as an overseas worker. Becoming TEFL certified. TEFL (Teach English as a Foreign Language) is a necessary qualification for the job literally spelt out in its initials. A friend of mine was considering taking the course and told me about it, as he knew I was like-minded and wanted to travel. We discussed possible locations while on the topic. He was drawn more to other European countries (Booooring) and admitted he doubted he could handle the drastic cultural changes that would come with living in Asia or South America. The same places I had my heart set on for those very reasons.

The qualification itself was pretty straightforward in theory. To pass, there was a module we had to finish online, which accounted for a percentage of our score and round off the course with a practical class. We were given access to the online portal in early April with the expectation to finish it by June. It would have been a straightforward process if my portal worked the whole time. I had to wait for an error in my account to be rectified by my Chinese representatives before I could start the course, which left me with three days to finish a course estimated to take 60 hours. As there are only 72 hours in 3 days, I was facing the colossal task of spreading 12 hours of sleep across three days to be able to finish this course on time. There was no time to panic.

There was no way I was going to fall short at this hurdle. I had come too far and invested too much time, resources, and money to stop here. As infuriating as it was, considering I was powerless and it was an issue I played no part in, the burden still rested on me to complete the course.

After isolating myself from the world in my bedroom, only leaving to eat or use the toilet, I managed to complete the course within the allotted time, to my relief. I could go back to allowing the excitement for the journey to come to flush away the angst and urgency that temporarily plagued me.

My relationship was also a massive pull in the direction of China. My girlfriend declared her plans to study in China while we were in the dating stage, roughly a year and a half before it was scheduled. We were barely in the position for her to change her plans in life for me, and I would never have asked her to. We kept seeing each other, and our feelings grew deeper, so I thought it was worth seeing where it went as a relationship. My rationale being I had never been in a relationship that lasted over a year before, so if we were still together by the time she had to leave, it might be something worth holding on to, even if it meant a lengthy separation. Luckily, I got the best of both worlds, and the gamble paid off handsomely.

I was already planning on moving abroad, so when the chance to join her in China presented itself, I felt like I had to take it. In the build-up to the trip, I grew more and more enthusiastic about the prospect of our relationship and the year I was going to spend exploring a new world with her. It was a prospect more exciting than any I had in memory. I could not think of a better way to spend my days than in her company. The idea of exploring the wonders of a new country with her beside me was a dream. Besides, both sets of our parents were a bit more at ease, knowing we had each other as a support mechanism whilst out there.

At the time that I agreed to the opportunity, I was unemployed. My days mostly consisted of looking for a graduate job after my last venture didn't work out. I was working as a Sports Coach as well as a Marketing Executive for a small company. With the coaching role feeling less fulfilling by the day and bearing an unsatisfactory level of income for the long-term, I decided to leave it behind.

The small company also looked like it was going to fizzle out, so I left before it met its inevitable fate. I was striking out in my job hunt at the time too. Most roles were looking for a graduate with a 2:1 or above within two years but had 12 years' experience. I only got a 2:2, and Sports Science degrees do not assist much with specialist employment.

I had no interest in returning to the world of education, so going back to complete a Master's course wasn't an option I was considering. I do enjoy learning and studying, but I have never felt like I ever maximised my potential within the confines of academia. I did not see the need to rush back to an environment I didn't feel I was thriving in, even if it meant better job prospects. It was becoming depressing, in all honesty. I had no idea what I wanted to do with myself, and I was being rejected for everything I put myself forward for. The euphoria from graduating and living my best life in South Africa was well and truly gone. Confusion and uncertainty weighed heavily on my existence, and I did not know how to put an end to it. To find clarity. Focus. A goal. Once I had confirmed my place teaching in China, I had one. Pass my TEFL course, jump the hurdles of documentation, and earn enough money to make it to China.

After around four months of unsuccessful job applications and pointless assessment days, I landed a Sales Executive job at a hospitality company to fund my journey despite it paying me a pittance of 12k basic salary for full time and beyond role. The commission was pretty good, however. In all honesty, if I did not need the job to fund my ambitions abroad, I would have quit on day one. I was plopped in front of a computer screen with names and numbers to call and a script of the pitch. The deep end became my home after a day's worth of practice. I hated everything about the role at first, and the thought of that being my life for six months terrified me. The contrast compared to the life I lived in South Africa was so stark. The rose-tinted glass that once reflected my life was shattering around me, leaving nothing but shards at my feet of memories that once were, an old Windows desktop, a phone, and a script on my desk. The ambitions that I withheld from my employer of making enough money to leave for China and quitting was the only reason I gave it a chance and eventually rose to the challenge.

I learned a lot from the role and began to excel at it, with every sale bringing me a step closer to Beijing. The problem was motivation slowly sapped away from my work ethic as time went on. I did not get paid commission until after the client paid meant I was racking up a considerable amount for future payments.

However, the commission wouldn't grace my account until after I would have left for China. Towards the end of my tenure, my employers noticed a considerable dip in what once was a tireless work ethic and called me in for a meeting. I was rather blunt in voicing my dissatisfaction with their payment scheme and admitted to running down the clock until the end of the month so that I could collect as much of the commission owed to me as possible. We agreed mutually to terminate my contract and pay me the commission I would have been due at the end of the month. Unfortunately, it was still 4-5k short of the overall commission I had earned there, but I didn't dwell on that for too long. The longer I stayed, the larger my phantom commission would have grown anyway.

As much as I'd learned and developed in the role, I still hated it. The buzz from making a sale is a euphoric high, but towards the end, where I knew I wouldn't see the financial benefit of the deals I made, it slowly became a hellish experience underpinned by crippling boredom. After saying my goodbyes to the sales floor, which I did grow quite fond of and vice versa, I had tears of joy welling up in my eyes. I had done it. I'd been through hell and back, but I'd done it! I slaved away at a job I could not stand and ventured far beyond my comfort zone to make enough money to get to Beijing, and I made it happen! I had left that job two months shy of my expected departure from London. As long as I didn't spend too much during that time, I was home free. Well, that's what I thought at the time. Some unexpected costs resulted in me dipping into my overdraft (and by dip, I mean maxing it out), but it did contribute the lion's share of costs, with the other fraction being fronted by donations from my immediate family, aunts, and uncles. For that, I will be forever grateful. This also included a £350 medical bill I didn't account for, as I missed the part in the paperwork where I had to prove my sound health to my would-be employers. I also needed to bring £500 worth of spending money to hold me until I got my first month of wages.

Those fees, along with all the other bits and bobs you could imagine I needed, accumulated to quite a hefty sum. Getting that medical was an ordeal in itself. I had to go to a specific medical centre in Brighton for some reason that escapes my memory. Well, two medical centres. One to give a urine sample to and the other to do a full-scale medical. As Brighton is pretty unfamiliar to me besides the tourist areas, I had to use my Maps app on my phone to navigate my journey. After a 30-minute bus ride, I found that I had mistyped the postcode and found myself at a hospital on the other side of Brighton. After discovering the right postcode, I caught a cab and a hefty bill to the correct location. They threatened to cancel the appointments for anyone who arrived more than 15 minutes late, so forking out for a cab was necessary. I spent that cab ride helplessly watching time escape me and wondering if my journey to China would end because a mistyped postcode caused me to piss in a tube too late. That wondering became more of a formality as I was 15 minutes late with over 10 minutes left of the ride left. My thoughts then travelled through whether I would charm my way into a late urine test or hope they pity the story of my traveller's woes. All I knew was that I could not take no for an answer. To my surprise, their threats of cancelling appointments late were empty. I gave them my name, and they walked me right through. What a relief!

Thinking all my troubles were over, after giving my sample, I walked down the road to have my medical, only to find the only doctor qualified to do my medical was not in the surgery. His absence was a rather massive shock to me as I'd emailed and called the doctor to confirm the time and date for my appointment. After I explained I had travelled from London, and it wouldn't be as simple as rescheduling for another day, I retrieved the doctor's mobile number to get to the bottom of the situation. Fortunately, he did not use his woefully booked day off to travel too far. I called him, and he was at home relaxing on his garden porch, which was no more than a 10-minute drive away. He apologised profusely and rushed straight over to carry out my medical. That simple day turned emotional rollercoaster would reveal itself to be a sign of things to come, in terms of near-misses and last-minute rearrangements, and I hadn't even stepped foot in China yet.

The visa also delayed things. I was advised not to book a flight until the visa was confirmed, but it was not until the week before I was due to arrive that it was. The prices for tickets skyrocketed from when I initially checked (approximately a month in advance). I had to borrow money from my Dad, so I could afford the flight over, secure in the knowledge I would be reimbursed at the end of my contract. I was extremely grateful, but it would have been preferable to have not had to resort to such measures.

Reactions

I knew it was a bombshell to drop on my family. With that considered, even though I knew it was confirmed, I said to them I was only considering it for the time being. I staggered the story when speaking about it to my parents and siblings because I did not want them to think I was making a rash decision. I stretched out the consideration, application process, getting the role, and deciding I was going to take it over the course of a month to give everyone a chance to digest what was happening and come to terms with the idea. I am not usually one for deception, but I had decided, and it was not up for debate. As much as I was not entirely comfortable with this method of breaking the news, it was the right one.

My group of closest friends all had mixed reactions. I will delve into my friendship dynamics in another chapter later in the book, but all I will say now is the ones who were genuinely happy for me are the ones I am still close friends with now.

My announcement of moving to China is still my most liked Facebook status to date. The majority of people were excited for me. It was a pretty surreal feeling having so many of your peers flooding you with support and messaging you good luck. People would almost be living vicariously through me as I kept them up to date with the latest events.

But Isn't China Racist?

People that cared about me were worried, as China has a bad reputation for racism. However, I have never been a person to let fear govern my actions, and I did not plan on beginning to allow it here. Yes, China does have a reputation for racism, but racism is everywhere, including the UK. I was also put at ease by how low the levels of violent crimes were in China, so if there was racism, I was assured it was highly unlikely to result in any immediate danger. A part of growing as a person involves pushing yourself outside of your comfort zone. If that zone resulted in the risk of experiencing racism, then so be it. I did not want to cower in fear and have regret hanging over my head in the future.

Why I Wrote the Book

I knew I would return to a barrage of questions, starting with the most dreaded and vague of them all, "How was China?" As if I could sum up an entire year of my life in a completely new country, immersed in one of the most unfamiliar cultures with a few concise sentences and give a satisfactory, well-rounded answer. I thought the best way to save myself the hassle it all was to write a book about the whole thing from start to finish. Leaving no stone unturned and allowing anyone interested to delve into my experience. The format I have chosen to do so is by sharing my memoirs—fortnightly entries summarising my experiences, feelings, and opinions on what had transpired within that time frame.

Scattered in between some of those updates will be articles highlighting differing subjects I wanted to scrutinise further. Some pieces are objective, while others are incredibly personal. I hope the end product of the words I have conjured has resulted in an enjoyable read.

Teacher's Training

After many months of anticipation, intense preparation, emotional farewells, and bracing myself for the oncoming cultural shockwaves, I finally arrived at Beijing International Airport on Saturday 15th August 2015. Trying not to let my jam-packed luggage and the fatigue from my 20-plus-hour journey weigh down my enthusiasm, I introduced myself to my guide and the other English teachers he would be escorting to our temporary residence, Capital Normal University. I was being helped with my luggage by a staff member, who suddenly had translation difficulties when I asked him if I had to pay for his services. Being fatigued, I just let him help me, only to find him gesturing for money once we reached my meeting spot. He pointed out a sign that had been hidden on the luggage trolley, showing me it cost 10 Yuan (about £1), which was worth it, to be honest. I was weary.

Being one of the later arrivals consequently meant I had no time to settle in my room. We dumped our luggage in the lobby so we could have dinner with the other teachers-to-be. By having dinner, I mean clumsily fumbling my chopsticks in an embarrassing attempt to feed myself. The locals I was seated with giggled with amusement while my fingers betrayed my appetite.

After the meal, I found out I had been paired with Jack, one of the other latecomers to share a hotel room. He was laid back, blonde, tall, and athletic. We couldn't follow the big crowd of people going to the bar/restaurant as we hadn't checked into our rooms. We had to take directions from another teacher and meet up with the rest of them later. After we had a quick look in our room and dropped our suitcases off, we headed off to find it. Our search resulted in a 25-minute walk when the place was meant to be around the corner. We had walked past it multiple times! The sun had set whilst we were inside. It was a lovely evening walk to soak up the feel of the place and get to know each other a little better. The site was on an upper level off a balcony, so we did not notice it while walking.

The atmosphere on the balcony was serene yet electric. The sense of excitement and optimism filled the air. We were all engulfed in conversations about the moments that lead to us all sharing this moment. We enjoyed the 70p bottles of beer while exchanging stories and comments regarding what we had hoped to gain from this journey. Reasons varied from wanderlust and the pursuit of a good time to more driven reasons such as learning Mandarin and testing the waters of teaching before committing to it back home.

Although it was tempting to make the most of the cheap beer, we were all well aware of the fact our teacher's training was set to commence in the morning. Most of us were drinking pretty moderately. The beer was pretty weak anyway, ranging from 3-5%. Once the clock hit midnight, we decided to head back to our room. I returned downstairs to utilise the Wi-Fi in the lobby to use WhatsApp to contact my family and my girlfriend to let them know I had arrived safely in China. Once I had finished, I snuck back into my room, being careful not to wake Jack. I did not sleep well. I kept waking up in a surreal state from the fact I was actually in China. I would have dreams where I was back home and then wake up here confused, having to remind myself where I was. Everything was happening so fast my mind had not fully processed it. I still cannot adequately articulate the feeling, but my mind was somersaulting. Me? In China. I spent so long preparing myself for this move, and now it was happening. I…was…here. It was such a different feeling to other occasions when I was abroad as I had just left home, and it was sinking in that I wouldn't be there again for nearly a year. My racing train of thought made it near impossible to drift into the deep slumber I desperately needed for the day ahead of me.

I was already exhausted by the time we had our 8 am lecture. The lack of sleep and jet lag was slowly lulling me into a mid-lecture nap. Not to mention I had bloated myself on some self-served generous portions from the breakfast buffet. Fortunately, the lecturer knew quite a few of us had only arrived the previous day and was familiar with how long-distance flights can affect your concentration. With that in mind, he made it clear he wouldn't take it personally if he saw anyone drifting off. That comforted me. Looking around to see several people losing the same fight for consciousness also eased any potential guilt. From what I had gleaned while I was awake, it was an informative lecture. I almost regretted falling asleep.

We had a lunch break before the next half of the lecture. The heat was scorching (30+ degrees Celsius), and I loved it. The brightness was extraordinary; I had never experienced such fierce sunlight. I could not go outside without squinting. Good thing my Mum strongly suggested I should get myself a pair of sunglasses and even gave me some money to go towards getting a decent pair. I opted for all black Ray-Bans, which would become a crucial accessory during sunny spells. I had never really been a fan of sunglasses as I always struggled to find a pair that suited me. These did the job aesthetically and practically.

I socialised a little during the break, but most people opted to find shelter in the shade and air-conditioned hotel lobby, to my disgust. And those who did stay outside refused to leave the shade. Heat close to this level had not embraced me since my family holiday to Jamaica in 2008. I was not going to run for cover now. I went for a slow walk around the campus to soak in those rays and observe their impressive facilities. The state-of-the-art buildings were in the presence of a generous amount of greenery. Lawns were maintained to perfection, and trees decorated pathways across the campus. It made tranquil scenery for my stroll. Alas, my enjoyment of my maraud was cut short. I needed to have lunch before making it back to class.

The second half of the lecture was mostly based on Chinese culture as opposed to teaching. The Lecturer went over some of the differences that may build-up to the "inevitable" culture shock—giving the context behind why they operate in such a manner and how to deal with individual circumstances. It was incredibly insightful. One thing I liked about the delivery of this lecture was the reiteration that we were not coming here as people from a "superior" culture, just a different one. We were told it was not our place to try and force our values onto people in this country but to observe and respect theirs. I feel that many British people have this mentality due to the country's colonial past, and it was vital for him to address that potentially surfacing. He also said it's only natural to see something you think is wrong and want to do something about it. He was using the example of public domestic abuse. In Chinese culture, if they see someone physically harming their significant other, they see it as rude to intervene, as it is not their business.

In contrast, most people culturally aligned with the Western Hemisphere would feel the need to try and defuse the situation. He admitted he struggled with that particular example himself and would expect us to as well. He wanted to make sure we knew that we should not expect a hero's reception from any onlookers if we decided to act in such a scenario.

Later that day, we were split into the groups we would be teaching in our summer camps, as well as finalising the pairs/threes we would be teaching in. I was placed in the Fengtai district, which I was glad to find was comprised of the majority of the people I had bonded with in the past 24 hours. My team was switched last minute due to a few people having yet to arrive in China for training, resulting in me having the pleasure of teaching with Golnaz. I had mixed feelings about this as I was initially in a group of 3, so I immediately knew my workload had increased. I'd also got to know Daniel, who was on my original team, reasonably well, and he was hilarious.

On the other hand, Golnaz was one of the first people I'd befriended as we'd met in London on our orientation day. We got along swimmingly too. The prospect of partnering with her was a good one. She shared my enthusiasm for teaming up. Well, why wouldn't she?

Team Fengtai had boarded our coach, which was taking us to our assigned district. This was the first time most of us had left Capital Normal since our arrival, aside from the place around the corner where we'd had a few beers. I sat at the back of the bus and soaked in all the views the Beijing roads had to offer. My positioning may have isolated me from the group, but for me, that was a price worth paying if it meant extra legroom. I was surprised by how undeveloped a lot of the City looked as we journeyed through. As the Capital of such a large nation, I expected the buildings to look considerably more modernised. Jaded-looking grey high-risers populated the majority of the roadsides and estates we drove past. They serve the purpose of giving homes to many in an overpopulated country, but the solution was not aesthetically pleasing in the slightest.

In contrast, the high streets were well decorated. Retailers and food chains were layered with huge signs decorated in neon lights with their luminous impact lost in the last hours of sunlight. I was under the impression that lacing neon lights all over aged buildings was a popular tactic for making them look more presentable.

Comments ricocheted around the coach about new observations as we journeyed through the terrain. The road laws were much laxer here. Families were packed onto motorbikes and scooters. Riders carried items on the back of buggies, ranging from logs to boxed merchandise, precariously placed and held down with makeshift strappings of ropes or elastic materials. One thing we all found collectively amusing was the habit some of the more overweight men had of rolling their t-shirts up to expose their bellies as a method of cooling down. Grown men with sizable guts were walking around looking like they were wearing belly tops, and it was a social norm. As childish as it may seem, it did not lose any comedic value with time.

We arrived after roughly an hour's journey at Beijing Fengtai No.8. University. We admired the university's facilities as we walked with our luggage through their grounds. They had a full-size astro-turf football pitch as well as basketball courts on the far side of the land. The main building also looked impressive. Further exploration would show they boasted an Olympic sized swimming pool.

I waited at the entrance with the other teachers at what would become our living facilities for the next ten days as we awaited the drafting of our dorm rooms as well as the distribution of our keys. I was paired with Peter. A tall, long-haired, Northern Irish heavy metal enthusiast who shared my love for Pokémon. Unfortunately, neither of us packed a link cable with our GameBoy Advance's, so there was no way of either of us asserting ourselves as the reigning Pokémon Master. I'm confident I would've wiped the floor with him, though; If my Vaporeon failed me, I'd let Charizard handle the rest. Our stay got off to a less than ideal start as a problem with our door handle left us locked out of our rooms. While all our peers were allowed to settle into their new digs, we were left in the hallway, standing by our luggage and getting to know each other. Eventually, the problem was solved, but unfortunately for us, it wasn't long before we were summoned to regroup with the others. Nothing like being stuck in a stuffy hallway to recharge after a long journey, right?

We were given a tour of the school and shown the classrooms we would be teaching in throughout our time there. We also had an absolute bombshell dropped on us that the one-hour classes we had prepared for before we flew out were three hours! Three sets of 50-minute teaching slots split up with 10-minute breaks. This revelation slapped us all in the face with a realisation. Even those of us who had thought we came prepared were 2 hours short of class content for each class. And we had two classes a day. This caused widespread panic among us as well as frustration. The consensus could not decide whether this was happening due to the ill-preparation of the training or the "last-minute change" culture we would become all too familiar with within China. Anyway, there was no time for feeling sorry for ourselves. With a painfully slow internet and limited resources, we had to get on with planning 6 hours' worth of material and hope to do so in time to get a decent night's sleep.

About 8 of us set up shop in Johnny and Theo's room to work together and conjure up some lesson content as well as share what we already had with each other. Johnny was one of the friendliest guys you could ever meet. He was a witty character, and seeing him without a smile was a rarity. His long dark hair and beard reminded me a bit of Andrea Pirlo. I never mentioned this to him, as I knew he had no interest in football, and the reference would've been wasted on him. I spent most of our time together fighting the urge to call him Pirlo.

Theo was an eccentric character whom you would have thought took a sworn oath to make himself the centre of attention everywhere he went. To be fair to him, he had the charisma to pull it off and became a favourite amongst us all, teachers and students alike. He reminded me a bit of Nathan from the show Misfits but less antagonising. A cheeky chappy but a charming bloke.

This lesson-planning hub was quite a success. Everyone left with a reasonably solid plan and more guidance with what we were going to do in the future. We shared our old notes and came up with new ideas together. Golnaz's laptop began a timely malfunction, handicapping her to only being able to help me out verbally. It also didn't help that she prepared nothing leading up to tonight so she had no prior notes to aid the cause.

The following day brought the first day of the Fengtai Summer Camp. It began with an opening ceremony in the main hall. We entered the hall and were greeted by a wave of excited giggles and whispers amongst the kids that would become our students for the next ten days. There were flag bearers on stage as well as music playing as we awaited the Principal's arrival. Following his speech, we were asked to stand on the stage where we were introduced to the crowd of children and then presented with our summer camp t-shirts. We were all given maroon-coloured t-shirts with the camp logo on them and a simple floral design on the bottom. We had the same shirts as the students, but they were all colour coded. The female students wore pink, and the males donned blue. A pretty early indicator of how much stereotypical gender roles would mould the social climate in China. I have never liked the concept of assigning genders to a colour, even in infancy. These kids were 15-16 with their identity being confined to a colour.

The gender separation mentality became more evident once we began teaching. As soon as Golnaz and I took our positions at the front of the class and the students were settled, we realised the boys all sat at the back or along the sides whilst the girls all sat at the front. We started by briefly introducing ourselves before getting straight into the icebreaker. We played two truths, one lie to get them talking and as a way for everyone, including ourselves, to tell the class something about themselves. As a whole, the class was still a bit timid, but it was a good start. We also got our two assistant teachers involved. Two women called Vivi and Sunni, who were a joy to work with.

We progressed into a game where everyone stood beside their desks, and we would ask them to keep standing if our statement related to them, e.g., keep standing if you are wearing a watch. I got my first glimpse of how prominent the one-child policy was when Golnaz said, "Keep standing if you have any brothers or sisters," and the entire class sat down. We looked at each other in amazement before one of the assistant teachers explained the one-child policy to us. We had heard of it before but had no idea it would be so effective or so strictly held. I had expected siblingless children to be more or less the norm but not to this extent. I had researched it in the past and found revelations of forced abortions and babies beyond the generous quota of 1 being murdered. But I had no way of being sure of how true they were. That moment was unofficial confirmation that those allegations just might hold some validity. I had no time to dwell on these thoughts now, though; I had a class to teach.

Our next phase was to split the group into 2, with Naz taking a group and myself taking another. We thought it would be an excellent way to get to know everyone a bit better and get them comfortable talking to us. The conversations were pretty stop-start from the beginning. I would ask a question and get very brief answers. I looked over at Golnaz's group and envied how her motor mouth was powering the conversation in her group. I was expecting more of an open chat where all the kids would chime in for an active group dynamic, but they only spoke when they were addressed and waited for me to come up with something. I had to get more creative with my questions as time passed, but it went ok. Naz and I swapped groups after a while, and this group was a bit easier to talk to. I think because they were mostly boys, they were more comfortable around me, and because when all else fails with a stereotypical man, you can always revert to sports. My basic knowledge of the NBA proved pretty useful in keeping conversations flowing as well as their intrigue of my background in football.

Once the icebreakers were over and we had to actually start teaching, we quickly settled into a good rhythm. Our chemistry worked well. Her talkative nature, combined with my reserved but assertive demeanour, provided a balanced mixture. Golnaz would break down the things that needed explanations before I stepped in to summarise each point concisely, giving the students a digestible format. We also got along nicely too. We bounced off each other's humour, giving the classroom an enjoyable show and laid-back atmosphere. We still had a bit of an issue getting the majority of the kids to open up, though.

It also helped us understand what we had to do for future lesson plans. In the preparatory stages of teaching, we were all given pretty abstract subjects to follow with our lesson content, which confused us. We realised once we got going that the subject was not the be-all and end-all. The main point was to get the students talking/reading/writing about the topic in English to practice communicating. Being experts or making the kids experts in the given topic was not necessary.

The evening sessions were a thing called "English Corner." It was more of an informal, laid back session. Although the whole day was pretty laid back due to it being the introductory session, the English Corner would maintain the more casual feel throughout the Summer

Camp. We played a game where we made them construct the adjectives we'd taught them earlier in the day into sentences. We had a ball we passed around and whoever had the ball had to start the sentence, e.g., "I am feeling upset because..." and then pass the ball to anyone of their choosing. Whoever caught the ball had to finish the sentence, e.g., "because I hurt my leg." And then start another sentence, "I am feeling excited because..." before passing the ball on to another player. We gave them a time limit to make sure the game didn't drag on and prohibited using the same word twice, forcing everyone to broaden their vocabulary as the game progressed.

This game proved to be a massive hit amongst all the kids and teachers alike, and embarrassingly, neither Golnaz nor I emerged victorious as we both got caught out by re-using a word previously said. Memory is far from my strongest asset, and it proved to be my undoing. At least I beat Naz, though. The class brainiac won the game. A girl who chose the English name "Thor." I loved her choice of name because she was the smallest girl in the class and chose the name of a powerful alpha-male warrior-god. It also shattered the gender norms that seemingly had a vice grip around this school's structure.

Day 2 had arrived, and there was still an air of awkwardness when trying to get some kids to answer the questions. To combat this, we introduced a points system, splitting the kids into two teams and rewarding a point for every correct answer. We also had a team for the Teachers, so if nobody gave us the right answer, the point would go to me, Naz, Vivi, and Sunni. We incentivised them by saying whichever team won the most days during the camp would get a prize on the last day. This gave the kids a new lease of life, turning the once withdrawn, disinterested kids into class enthusiasts, raising their hands in the air hoping to be selected to answer questions. We made sure we picked out the less enthusiastic ones of the group now and then to ensure every child made some sort of contribution to each class.

As we all taught our classes in pairs and some in threes, members of each teaching group were given alternate days off to enjoy a day of tourism while those left behind had to continue a day of teaching back at the university. On our day out, we had the pleasure of being guided around the Temple of Heaven and Earth.

Our trip was, however, somewhat marred by our supervisor dropping a bombshell on us. We would have a surprise exam to return home to. Failure to pass would result in the failure of the TEFL course, invalidation of our visas, and our forced return to our native lands. Understandably, the news caused quite a few people in our group to panic or ended up partially distracted from our visit. Others could recall us being warned of this in our opening lectures back at Capital Normal University. Either my poor memory was failing me again, or I slept through that part. Either way, it was an unexpected, unwelcome surprise. I didn't allow myself to be nervous. I'd invested too much time and had spent too much money to turn back now. By hook or by crook, I was here to stay. I went into full-blown tourist mode and made sure I enjoyed the trip without distraction. We had a guide showing us the main attractions of the place. Meanwhile, we were becoming the main attraction to other native tourists, as expected. During our preparation for this venture into the heart of East Asia, we have all had the fact drilled into the forefront of our cerebrums that we would stand out amongst the native people. We would stumble upon "celebrity status" where our physical presence alone will be enough to make grown adults giggle like children, fixate on you with a gaze of awe and wonder as well as take pictures of you, with or without your consent. We got a pretty hefty sample of the kind of attention we had been getting once we were unleashed in our stationed cities. It was pretty hilarious. I would be reading placards explaining the history of an ancient artefact and how its story had been woven into the nation's history. Yet, for some reason, people deem me as the more exciting discovery worth capturing on camera. I was approached for photos by men, women, groups of friends, families, the lot. There was a moment where a small queue had formed for me. I had strangers giving me their babies to hold for photos. A guy even ushered me towards his family, and he took a picture of us with my arm around his partner and his children. They were my family now.

The last stop on our journey was the highly anticipated trip to Tesco. My primary objective was to find some decent skin cream and hair-care products. I made the absent-minded and costly error of packing what was meant to be my year's supply of those products into my hand luggage, forcing me to leave it all at the security checks and giving it to my parents. Learning of Tesco's presence in China gave me hope this mistake would not be too fatal for my skin's moisture level.

Unfortunately, I could not find anything that didn't contain skin-whitening agents. As someone who takes pride in his luxuriously dark melanin filled complexion, I did not deem those as a viable option. I had to continue making the pocket-sized skin creams I bought in the airport and was given in-flight and stretch them until further notice. Luckily, the temperature in Beijing at the time rarely dipped below 30 degrees Celsius, so I didn't need a lot to get me through the day. The natural oils from my skin mixed with the light sweat guaranteed in these conditions ensured I never had an ashy day.

I managed to find a decent shampoo and conditioner. The only reason I trusted it was because the packaging looked similar to Tre-Semme, which I knew was reliable from using it back home. I also bought some cheap shorts. In all the preparation for this journey, the one thing I did not think to bring was a pair of casual shorts, although I knew the sweltering Beijing summer heat awaited me. I managed to find some plain grey elastic-waisted casual shorts that did not look short on my ridiculously long legs, to my pleasant surprise. Not what I would usually go for, but beggars can't be choosers.

I was meant to buy snacks for the kids, according to Golnaz, but I was unaware of this due to either not being told, being told and not listening, or having problems with my recollection again. Honestly, it was probably one of the latter two. Everyone else was stacking up on western snacks they had been craving seemingly since their planes had elevated from British soil. I honestly was not particularly fussed. It had only been about a week, and at the time, my appetite did not live up to its usual standards. I discovered later on that a loss of appetite is an effect of jetlag. I thought once I got my body's clock right, I would be home free, but I was wrong. I also wanted to save money. I only had limited funds until my first wage instalment as a teacher, so spending on home culinary comforts was not a priority. I did not fly all this way to buy snacks I could have gotten from my local corner shop. Not this early into the trip anyway. We returned to campus and began preparing for the exam, which we had managed to acquire the questions for. To our relief, the questions were mostly multiple-choice. An even more significant relief was the exam would be open book, easing the group's collective fears of deportation. To our relief, the questions were mostly multiple-choice. An even more significant relief was the exam would be open book, easing the group's collective fears of deportation.

We had also covered the vast majority of the questions either in our lectures or during the online modules of the course. A group of us prepared the necessary notes for our exam, which we all passed comfortably. The next day I had to teach the class alone, as Naz had her turn to indulge in tourist activities. It was straightforward, especially as I had Vivi and Sunni to help me out. A highlight of that day was them asking me to teach them the longest word in the English language, and I gave them antidisestablishmentarianism to master.

It became a class competition to see who could spell it correctly or get the closest. Unsurprisingly, Thor was the first to spell it correctly, taking the points home for her team. I thought I would spice things up a bit and allow them to teach me some Chinese words and phrases. The most notable word was "biang" which was a popular noodle-based meal originating from Xi'an. It doesn't look like much in the Pinyin translation (Pinyin is spelling Mandarin words with the English alphabet). Still, it is the hardest word to write in the Mandarin language, according to my students. One of my students drew the word on the chalkboard for me to replicate and set the challenge off, which I somehow managed to do. I can barely write intelligible words in English, let alone Mandarin. I had to leave the afternoon class early so I could coach football. With Naz gone, they were left in the capable hands of Vivi and Sunni.

In terms of how I started coaching football in an English Teaching academy came to fruition, Naz and I had spoken to Sabrina and Theo a couple of days prior. They had told us their assistant teachers were becoming flexible with the lesson planning. They didn't have to follow the syllabus strictly and were even allowed to take their class outside.

Hearing that and warming to the idea of taking our class out into the glorious heat, we asked our supervisor, Nikki, if we could do the same. However, I got a lot more than I signed up for. As soon as I asked, a light bulb flashed in Nikki's head as she paired my face with my CV and realised I was "the one with the resume," i.e., the Level 2 football coach. Once she confirmed who I was, she went full steam ahead with setting up an extracurricular football session for anyone who wanted to join.

Within 10 minutes, they printed off permission slips for the children to have signed, arranged logistics with me, and were eager to get the show on the road. I was taken aback by how quickly they had put everything in place. I also considered the fact I usually charged for these services and thought about the prospect of negotiating. However, it would have taken me out of the classroom for an hour or so, and I was excited about the possibility of coaching football in China. I let them have the freebie.

I also had Adam to run the session with. Adam is a Sunderland native and a fan of the team, made evident by him wearing their famous red and white stripes when meeting for the first time. He was also a football coach, so he was approached to help with this rapidly forming mini- academy. We bounced ideas off each other concerning drills we could do with the kids, although we wouldn't directly be working together. Nikki put me in charge of the 10th graders and Adam with the 8th graders. It was tough as we had a minimal idea of the resources we'd have to use or how many kids would sign up, or how good they would be as this was all being sorted on the spot! We assumed we wouldn't be working with any elite players and formulated simple drills we could expand or downsize depending on how many kids we had.

We were left with over 50 kids between us to coach. Our resources were a football pitch we were going to split in half. It also had two small goals on either by-line that would come in handy for playing matches. Additionally, we had eight footballs (4 for me, 4 for Adam) and ten traffic cones (yes, traffic cones) to use as markers (5 each).

Surprisingly, I had the lighter load as more 8th grade children signed up. I lead the warm-up as well as the stretches to kick things off. Once everyone was limber, I used the few cones I had at my disposal to set up some basic dribbling drills to gauge the quality of players I was working with. As we guessed, it wasn't great. This made my job easier as I could keep the drills basic and challenging for them at the same time, which helped, as my resources were limited. After the dribbling, I progressed into simple passing drills where they would get into groups of 5 or 6 before making a circle. That also went smoothly. From there, we moved into a match. To my surprise, one of the kids wanted to opt-out of the match and kept practising his passing. I told him to join in, but he didn't feel comfortable yet, so I let him practice his ball control on the side-lines.

The second and last session was a lot more laid back as Adam and I both knew what we were working with. We did few football-related competitions (i.e., the first group to string 20 passes together/the first team to complete ten headers.) before going straight into matches. The game in my last session was congested, so I decided to split them into three teams with a winner staying on rule. If matches were tied after 5 minutes, I would pick a team to go off. In the half an hour of the matches being played, only one goal was scored, meaning I had to do the latter. The goal was surprisingly brilliant; a long-range free-kick scored by a boy who picked the unorthodox name of "Rank." He was also in my English class, and we bonded over football throughout our time at the camp.

Football also managed to seep into class during English lessons. My love for Chelsea became somewhat contagious. I managed to turn the whole class into fanatics. One boy decided to call himself Chelsea because he had yet to choose an English name, unlike most English-speaking Chinese students. Coincidently, he was one of the two kids I bonded with the most. Chelsea was a gifted basketball player despite his lack of height, possessing some of the best handles I'd seen, and we spent much time alternating between playing football and basketball together.

Education aside, we had to prepare our class for the closing ceremony performance, where we let the students decide what we were going to perform. They opted for an upbeat rendition of Mark Ronson and Bruno Mars's "Uptown Funk," followed by the more emotive and timely choice of Wiz Khalifa's "See You Again." We were fortunate enough to have two gifted dancers in our class who took it upon themselves to choreograph the Uptown Funk performance. However, we did have to step in and give simpler alternatives for those dancers who weren't as rhythmically gifted. In the last 4 or 5 days of the Summer Camp, all the teachers used the time allocated to our evening English Corner to rehearse for the ceremony.

Golnaz and I had a cameo in the show. We joined in for the last part of the routine, which was a nice touch. We also incorporated what was originally me blowing off steam with Chelsea by doing football tricks while he showed off his basketball handles in our class breaks. Chelsea used to throw me the basketball after dribbling it, and I would start doing kick-ups with it. The rest of the class thought us replicating this on stage would be a great way to round off Uptown Funk. It slotted in perfectly and was a massive hit with the crowd on the day of our performance.

After the performances, we were all ushered out of the hall in a brisk fashion, and we all broke into a light jog into the playground. At the time, none of us teachers had a clue what was happening. We were on what I could only explain as a victory lap around the playground with all the students. I recorded some of it on my phone while running backwards and toppled over one of the smaller goals placed on the by-line! Once all of us were outside, we grouped back into our classes, embraced each other, and spoke about the performances. A sense of exhilaration filled the air. The energy was electric. There were hundreds of us on the football pitch, buzzing from our performances and energised from our run. Everyone's face was emblazoned with smiles, and excited chatter could be heard in all directions.

However, the feeling slowly drained away. It dawned on us that it was the last evening we were ever going to spend with each other. I noticed some of the kids looking towards Golnaz and me with tears in their eyes. We acted quickly on consoling those in need of it, sharing hugs and reassuring words to all of those who needed it.

As it was our last day of camp, we had a party to celebrate. We managed to get hold of a decent amount of alcohol, and we all congregated in one of the dorm rooms. None of us had touched any alcohol since we left Capital Normal, so we were excited by the prospect of a strong beverage. It was a rare opportunity for all of us to let our hair down and socialise properly. Besides the day trip and mealtimes in the canteens, we didn't get too many opportunities to do so. We worked all day practically and used all of our spare minutes planning the next day's lessons. This was a welcome change from the intensity that held us all captive for the duration of the summer camp. Drinks flowed as freely as the conversation and laughter filling the room. The warm sense of euphoria and accomplishment embraced us all. We'd done it!

On our final morning, we all had parties in our respective classrooms. We played music, awarded the class who achieved the most points, had snacks, and just had fun. Chelsea and I had one more freestyle session, with him showing off his basketball tricks and me doing the same with the ball at my feet. It felt quite dreamlike, knowing I would never do this with him again. I experienced emotive recollections of fond memories while enjoying the very moment we were sharing. I felt like I had an idea of what it felt like for an athlete to play their last game for a team. Knowing every action you are currently doing, with the people you are doing it with and having gotten so accustomed to, was also among your last. It transcended the present moment in a joyous yet depressing manner.

We had a great time. What I enjoyed most was seeing the growth amongst the children Golnaz and I taught. The range of personalities that blossomed under our tutelage was a joy to behold. Their willingness to grasp the English language also made our jobs as educators much more manageable and enjoyable. We found the right balance of work and play pretty early, which helped retain their attention throughout the camp. Ours mirrored Their growth. Within that time, we felt like accomplished teachers, confident in our personalities and abilities to rise to the challenge ahead.

The collective enthusiasm from the students and teachers alike bounced off each other wonderfully to produce an excellent environment for everyone.

After ten days with those children, we felt like a family, which made saying goodbye a challenging task. They were our kids. On our departure, the students gave a guard of honour to all the teachers, and we walked through with heavy luggage and even heavier hearts. We embraced our students for the last time. There were many well wishes, and tears flowed from teachers and students alike, while the burden of masculinity made me fight tooth and nail to hold mine back. I decided to take my sunglasses off, so I could fully convey my emotions to the kids. I was choked up and teary-eyed from the prospect of leaving them behind, but I wanted them to see how much they meant to me, just as their tears did that for me. We climbed onto the coach and clambered to the one side of the coach so we could wave to our kids one last time.

It was not the last of our farewells. The teachers who were based in Shanghai were on a different schedule to us. They had to go straight to their destinations to sort out their accommodation. We said our goodbyes to the Shanghai squad before they bundled off the coach at Beijing Station to embark on their adventure.

The rest of us returned to Capital Normal University. The university would once again become our base for the next two days while we enjoyed some of Beijing's world-famous tourist attractions. This would be the first time since arriving in China where we would have time to relax genuinely. No worries about lesson planning. No concerns about taking notes from teacher training lectures and, most importantly, no more surprise exams. Just seeing the sights by day and enjoying ourselves by night.

We got to choose our roommates this time around. I roomed with Daniel. He's still to this day probably one of the funniest people I have ever met. He was also one of the very few Manchester United fans I knew who was actually from Manchester.

After dropping off our luggage, we embarked on what was the second walk I'd had in this area, with my first walk being with Jack on the night I landed. This one I got to enjoy fully. We were genuinely exploring as opposed to getting lost and hopelessly looking for a destination. I managed to find a shop that resembled a pharmacy, so I looked for a moisturising skin cream. My pocket-sized moisturiser was wearing dangerously thin, and I needed something. Out of desperation, I bought their top of the range natural skin cream, according to what the shopkeeper via his translation app was telling me. I assumed "natural" would mean an absence of skin lightening agents, so I jumped at the chance to buy it. With the exchange rate of the GBP to RMB still fuzzy in my mind, I didn't realise until I'd left the shop that I had paid approximately £10 for a pretty small tube. I was used to getting bottles of cocoa butter five times the size for half the price, so I felt a little hard done by. Daniel and I both joked and said I should start walking around naked to show off my radiant skin and get value for money!

We stopped off at an open restaurant in one of the back streets off the main road. The place was a lot safer and more legitimate than my description of the location would lead you to believe. We had a couple of cheap beers and relaxed. We noticed a man sitting across the room from us doing the same with his son, who could not have been any older than 2. This didn't stop him from taking a sip of beer from his dad's glass, though. We watched in astonishment as this toddler casually held the glass of beer his dad handed him and sipped like it was Ribena. He didn't even flinch at the taste, which made me guess this was not his first time. I knew the beer was weaker than it was back in the UK and that there was no minimum drinking age, but I was still taken aback. I did not think I would see anyone become acquainted with alcohol before the alphabet.

Night fell, and we went out as a group for the first time. I thought we were going to the same place we had beers on the first night, so I dressed super casual, wearing cheap shorts I bought from Tesco and a plain white tee. I got downstairs to see everyone else dressed in smart-casual wear. Shirts, dresses, the works! I asked why I did not get the memo, and Daniel responded by saying it's because they had to compete with my good looks somehow. The man had a point.

We walked down the road and into one of the most luxurious shopping malls I'd seen. We headed for KTV, which is a host to private karaoke rooms you can rent out with a group of your friends. Each room usually has multiple televisions, microphones, and tablets for you to choose the songs you wanted to sing along to. We got the celebrity foreigner treatment we were warned about before arriving, and we loved every minute of it. We were giving their best room free of charge, as well as three crates of beer for us to help ourselves to.

Before we started singing, I found myself with one of the microphones in my hand. For some reason, everyone wanted me to do a speech. I started strong before trailing off and ad-libbing the rest, trailing off into repetition and empty buzzwords.

I showed off my talents on stage more than I'd planned because people were hesitant to go up. Quite a few songs were being selected that I knew, and nobody was grabbing the microphone. I kept the ball rolling and grabbed it myself. This worked in my favour as the night went on as I was practically repaid by being allowed to be more selfish with my song selections later on in the night, including Rich Homie Quan's song, "Flex (oooh ooh ooooh)," which was my favourite song of that summer. Little did I realise, as many times as I had hit the Dougie to that song while having it on repeat, I hardly knew any of the words. This resulted in a hilariously poor rendition when I grabbed the microphone. It also did not help that I was the only person in the room that had even heard the song. I still had a blast dancing around to it, though!

The next morning, we were setting off to The Great Wall. The more disciplined of us kept this in mind during our night at KTV and didn't get too carried away with the booze, and managed to get a decent night's sleep. Others weren't so forward-thinking and went all out that night, and it didn't take long for the effects of their poor decision to show, starting with a few of the boys arriving late for the coach looking like extras from The Walking Dead. They trudged towards their seats and fell asleep instantly. On arrival, they decided on taking the easier route up the wall at a minimal pace while the rest of us trudged up the steeper part of the wall. The more physically demanding way was rewarded with breath-taking views at the summit.

In the evening, a group of us went to KTV again. It was a smaller group than last time, and we shared the room with another group of English teachers. There wasn't as much chemistry in terms of music tastes, and people kept changing the track midway through performances, which was annoying, especially as some people who didn't contribute to paying for the room were doing it. I grabbed the microphone and warned anyone who had not contributed financially to refrain from skipping songs. At times we had to grab people's hands to stop it from happening. In protest, I performed Bobby Shmurda's "Bobby Bitch" as I knew the meddlers in the other group would hate my selection.

The next morning, I was woken up early by Daniel's exit. He had a gruelling 36-hour train ride ahead of him to his destination, so he was understandably in the earliest group of departing people. We said our goodbyes before he headed downstairs. When I was settling back into my bed, I saw in my peripheral vision a dangling wire by his bedside, which happened to be Daniel's phone charger. Realising this, I woke myself up properly and put on some shorts so I could catch Daniel before he left. It's not like he could pop down to Curry's and buy a new one. Especially at the distant location he was heading. I saw someone from our group which I never really got to know, hence me not remembering his name, but I knew he would know Daniel, so I passed on the charger to him as he was entering the lift. On my way back to my room, I bumped into Priyanka, who was lugging a suitcase that looked bigger than her (she's about 5ft). She asked me to help her out so I carried her luggage to the lift and hugged her goodbye, making my way back to my room in the hope I could return to my slumber, uninterrupted by any more forgetful packers or people struggling with luggage.

A few hours later, I was reawakened by my phone alarm, which signalled my last morning in Beijing. Once we all made it to the lobby, we received our TEFL certificates; the physical manifestation of our efforts in the Summer Camp paying off, and the official validation of our status as Foreign Language Teachers. For me, it was also a reminder of the three days I locked myself in my bedroom to finish the online modules before the deadline. It was not a very ceremonial moment; we had to swiftly put our certificates away in our luggage and prepare to get on the coach. The Beijing train station awaited us, and so did our new home cities for the year.

We braced ourselves for the next chapter, where we scattered across the country to our host cities, ready to begin our stint as official English teachers. I was already looking back in awe of what I'd experienced in a life-changing fortnight. But with so much ahead of me, I must also keep looking forward. Although the adventure had been euphoric so far, it was only the beginning…

Welcome to Changzhou

After a 6-hour train ride (a surprisingly pleasant experience as the seats were comfy, legroom was abundant, and the air conditioning was crisp), I was greeted at the train station by Daniel. I finally got to see the person behind some of the emails I received to coordinate this placement. He was pretty tall, about 6'1 with a slight frame. He also wore glasses. He was nice enough to help me with one of my bags, but I still had my work cut out with my hefty suitcase as the handle had broken off, making it awkward to manoeuvre. It did not help that the car was parked a fair distance from the station. After 5 minutes of dragging my handle-less luggage down the road, I was greeted by a small woman with whom I exchanged smiles with as a greeting. We had no common lingual ground, so this would be the extent of our communication.

She conversed with Daniel in Mandarin for the majority of the journey. Their voices gradually faded into background noise as I stared through the window, absorbing the new terrain. Honestly, there wasn't much to absorb. We mostly drove past barren fields and aged high risers with small shops and market stalls littered between them. The route we had driven worried me. I may have made a mistake in picking Changzhou as my location. I was initially offered a role in a slightly bigger and better-known town called Suzhou, where quite a few of the friends I had made in the camp were staying. I opted for Changzhou because the school allowed me to teach P.E in addition to English, which appealed to my coaching background. They also paid more than the role in Suzhou, which was always going to turn my head. Another plus for me was the location was closer to Nanjing, where my girlfriend would be staying. Now I was having second thoughts, wondering if the perks I signed up for were in exchange for living in a ghost town.

We pulled up to the place I would call home for the next year. Wujin Qinying Foreign Language School. We drove through an impressive compound and parked outside the living quarters. I was coldly welcomed by five flights of stairs I had to scale with my luggage, seeing as there were no lifts in the building. I did have a rose waiting for me on my bed once I made it to the room. It lay beside a friendly welcome note and a Ferrero Rocher, a sweet gesture from my hosts.

I relieved my arms of the weight of my luggage and sat on my bed. That feeling of relief was relatively brief, as my bed felt like I was sitting on wood. After closer inspection, my heart dropped when I realised I was. The "mattress" was a wooden platform coated in a thin layer of what I think was wool and nylon. I didn't allow myself to dwell on it for too long. This was what I signed up for. It was just an unexpected adjustment as the hotel/university beds I had slept on for the past two weeks all had mattresses I was accustomed to.

Daniel shortly came back with a massive bottle of water for my dispenser as well as a Wi-Fi router before offering to show me where I would have dinner. Upon leaving my room, Daniel and I walked into a rush of people heading down the corridor, and he told me to follow them to the lunch hall, saving him the burden of escorting me. They were a group of 20+ North American teachers who would also be living on campus. I had no idea until then that any overseas teacher would accompany me. I was startled yet excited by the prospect of having some company.

The onslaught of American accents alerted me to the fact that I would be the only person here flying the flag for the UK. They welcomed me with open arms, and I integrated pretty quickly, considering the circumstances. I was winding down from a 7-hour journey, contemplating how I would navigate through these unfamiliar lands as a lone wolf, to being thrown into a sea of Americans whose current was gently but briskly, carrying me to what would be my place of dining for the forthcoming year. One thing that would take more time to get used to was the last-minute culture of China. You would think the fact I would be part of a community of foreign teachers within the school would have reared its head into the discussion somewhere along the line.

I struck up conversations with 2 of the teachers who introduced themselves to me. They were Jadden (pronounced Jaden) and Alexis. The spotlight on me began to pick up its intensity once it became apparent I was English. I got my fair share of "Oh my God, you're British!" exclamations in my direction, followed by introductions, niceties, and further conversation as we headed for the dinner table. We were served fried chicken with fried rice, which was a nice, familiar introductory meal. While we ate, I spoke more to Jadden and Lexie and met Heidi and Devin, a married couple previously residing in Utah. Straight off the bat, Devin made his passion for film the forefront of the conversational topic by asking if I shared the interest and who my favourite directors were. Although I do love a good movie, I would hardly describe myself as a film geek, but at the same time, I did not want to blurt out an obvious choice such as Tarantino, Spielberg, or Scorsese. I revealed my recent liking to Wes Anderson movies, which garnered his approval.

After further conversation, I found out that all the American teachers were part of the same agency, which sends volunteer English teachers to foreign countries. They arrived in Changzhou roughly two days before me and quickly used those days to get to know the area a little better, offering to show me around whenever they could. That filled me with relief as the drive from the train station to the school gave me the impression I was in the middle of a concrete abyss. All I saw were huge roads and high risers with very little activity, so the chance to ride their coattails around Changzhou was golden for me.

Later that day, Jadden knocked on my door to invite me down for Ping-Pong with some others in the group. I was doing pretty well for myself before Maryn, a petite blonde woman, nonchalantly picked up a paddle and effortlessly killed me within the first two shots of each rally we had. Of all the trials and tribulations I was expecting on this journey, I was not expecting to feel at my most powerless at the opposite side of a ping pong table of someone half my size. I gave up my paddle in defeat and started to get to know some of the other group members. I only spoke to 3 or 4 of them in any real depth during dinner, so it was an excellent chance to break the ice with a few more. I did not stick around for too long. I was shattered, and my wooden bed was calling my name. Its siren song lacked the seductive cadence of my bed at home, but the fatigue seeping through my body made me appreciate it nevertheless.

The next morning moved pretty slowly. I spent the morning with a few of the American teachers basking in the summer heat and slowly roaming around campus. It was not as hot as the eye squinting sunrays of Beijing, but the temperature was still comfortably in the late 20's, and I was enjoying every moment.

At lunch, I saw a free seat available next to some faces I was yet to bump into, so I took a seat and introduced myself. They were two friends, Alesha and Jacqueline. They also arrived on campus the day before me and, to my relief, revealed there was a lot more to the city than what I had seen on the journey to Wujin. They announced their plans of going into town later that day and asked if I would like to join their group. I jumped at the chance. I wanted the opportunity to see the place for myself and put my concerns to bed. I had also never been out in this country by myself, and I had no intention of my first time being at a time where I had no idea where anything was. They also told me about what sounded like the promised land of Changzhou's cuisine. They spoke incredibly highly of a night market that was about a 10-minute walk from us.

The ride into town introduced me to a livelier, more developed side of Changzhou that I was excited to see. High streets were alive with neon signs and densely populated. There were also many malls. Some were open for business, and others were under construction. There always seemed to be construction work going on somewhere. I saw the logos of global brands I was familiar with as well as Chinese brands I had never heard of. However, their grandeur was not lost on me as the size of some of their stores were rather impressive as well as their billboards. Their neon signs dominated high streets and the sides of shopping malls, making their unmistakable marks as commercial powerhouses.

In all honesty, once we got to the town centre, it was a blur. There was so much to take in. I was walking through the similar high streets I passed on the bus, as well as several stalls selling food or other merchandise. The streets were alive with shoppers pacing towards their next retail destination. I wasn't looking to buy anything on this occasion as I didn't want to over-exert my finances before I got paid my first month's salary. Still, I spotted a Tesco as well as a Wal-Mart that I planned on re-visiting if I ever needed any Western snacks and appliances. I was expecting to do many things in China for the first time, but I didn't think for a second that shopping in Wal-Mart would be part of that list.

It was an enjoyable excursion. I returned home awash with a much-improved knowledge of Changzhou and of the colleagues I came out with. I was now considerably more optimistic and excited about what life would be like for me here.

Later that evening, I was sitting on the side of my bed whilst on my laptop before I got a knock on the door. It was unlocked, so I shouted for the knocker to come in. Daniel's head appeared around my door and said another teacher had arrived. He asked if the newcomer could stay with me until his key was sorted. I agreed. Moments later, a casually dressed guy rolled his suitcase into the corner of his room and removed his headphones from around his neck. My face lit up, and I filled with enthusiasm. It was another black guy!! I had seen only 4 or 5 in the Beijing market, but I hadn't been able to interact with any, and this one was going to be my neighbour. He shared the same enthusiasm when he saw me, and we greeted each other with handshakes and smiles before I offered him a seat. His name was Anthony, a 27-year-old who resided in New Jersey before making the trip out here. He had a decorated educational and business background. Our sense of humour seemed pretty compatible from the start, and we shared quite a few laughs in the 5 minutes he was in my room. Daniel returned with Anthony's key, and he went to his room to unpack and settle into his new place. I was hoping this was the start of a beautiful friendship.

The following afternoon, all the foreign teachers, consisting of Anthony, the 20+ ILP teachers and myself. On arrival, we were greeted with fast-food takeaway style cups of milk tea. This was the first of many milk teas we all had, as it almost instantly became a favourite beverage amongst us. It's pretty much like bubble tea, but without the bubbles and milkier. We gathered in the boardroom and awaited the arrival of Cathy. She was the head of the Foreign Language department and the other person I had been liaising with via email. She was the one who scouted my CV and offered me a contract here. Another face I was looking forward to associating with a name. She arrived and introduced herself to us, reassuring us she would always be there to support us whenever we needed anything and we should see her as our mother figure during our stay, which was endearing. We went on to discuss basic house rules such as curfews. Mine and Anthony's curfew on school nights was midnight. The ILP teachers had an earlier curfew,

11 P.M. They also weren't allowed to leave the campus unless they were at least in pairs. They had more restrictions because of the ILP group's internal regulations and because they were volunteers. Anthony and I got friendly enough with the security guards for them to overlook our curfews. We showed them pictures of us at Chinese tourist attractions as well as us trying on Chinese robes. This translated as us embracing China and everything the country had to offer, which is practically a personal compliment over there. The collectivist culture ensues any praise or criticism of the country as a whole can be taken personally by the majority of Chinese people—something we used to our advantage despite the language barrier. We would often arrive to see sleeping guards operating the gates. We would sneak back in carefully, not to wake them out of consideration for their beauty sleep as opposed to fear of consequences.

We also spoke about the basics they would expect from us as teachers and laying down some basic ground rules. Cathy was even lovely enough to allow us the first week off to allow us to settle into our new home.

Once the meeting was finished, we were sent upstairs to prepare our classrooms, which had been pre-assigned. After a brief period of following the other teachers around, I realised the classroom preparation orders did not apply to me and only applied to the ILP teachers. I'd also realised Anthony was absent from the crowd of teachers, which probably meant he realised the same thing as I did but a little quicker. I chased after Cathy only to find out Lily was the person I should be talking to. After finding Lily, she scrambled around to find my schedule and had a bombshell dropped on me. I, as well as Anthony, would start teaching tomorrow. After a glance at my timetable, I realised they had crammed my schedule with far more than the agreed 18 lessons a week I signed up for in my contract. They had also said to me previously that I had to assist football coaching sessions starting at 6:30 am from Monday – Friday, which I clarified also counted as lessons. I flagged that to both Cathy and Lily. They quickly adjusted my timetable to 15 classes and said I only have to do three football sessions (Tuesday, Wednesday, Thursday). Who would have thought I would need to ask for my contract to be honoured? Or need to use my initiative to find out when I started teaching?

Considering I was starting the next day, I was given the task to find my classes. In China, (with ILP Teachers being the exception) the teachers aren't assigned classrooms here, the classes are. The teachers have to move between classrooms. I was also slowed down by the numbers being written in Mandarin. I had to ask another teacher what everything meant, and he taught me a fool proof way to understand them while poorly disguising laughter at my struggle. I guess he found it entertaining that I failed to understand the simplest of Chinese numeracy, but I shrugged it off. Anthony and I had to find our classes. I would see him flitting from room to room while I was trying to scout classroom doors. I had yet to find every class, but I figured out enough of the classes to piece together where each year group was. After knowing that and with my newfound ability to read the Mandarin numbers on my schedule, I was confident in my ability to make it to my classes on time.

On my way back to my room, I bumped into Cathy. We had a brief exchange, and she told me to meet her on the field at 8 am the next day. I had been given the impression it would be a casual pep talk before I began my teaching career, so I dressed as such, in a t-shirt and shorts. The weather was still in the late 20 degrees Celsius. Once I arrived there, it was the complete opposite. The entire school was out on the field grouped in their classes with their teachers. I spotted Anthony and the ILP teachers grouped with everyone dressed in smart clothing. Shoes, trousers, ties, dresses, skirts, the works! They told me today was the opening ceremony for the school year, hence their attire. I explained to them all I was told was to meet Cathy here. They found it as hilarious as I did bewildering. I was in disbelief that she never thought to mention the fact a ceremony was taking place. I did feel more relieved when I looked around and saw whom I guessed were PE teachers dotted around the area in sportier-looking clothing. As I taught PE and English, I comforted myself by thinking I too could be considered appropriately dressed.

All the foreign teachers were made to line up in front of the school as a presentation, reminiscent of the summer camp ceremony. We were all handed two t-shirts (one yellow, one orange) with the school logo on the back. For me, those were the two absolute worst colours to give me, as they are probably the only two I actively dislike wearing. Once the school had their time of smiling and waving at the new foreign teachers, Anthony and I cleared off while the ILP teachers stayed on to do an unforgettable dance performance. Their song of choice was the smash hit "Whip/Nae Nae" by the teen sensation and artistic descendant of Soulja Boy, Silento.

When the whole ceremony was over, all the foreign teachers were again pulled aside for group photos that ended up on the school's wall of foreign teacher groups. Then came the teaching.

I did not have ideal preparation, but I managed, and my classes all ran smoothly. In my first PE session, Cathy assured me that I would play the role of assistant to a Chinese teacher, until I got into the swing of things, only for me to be left outside, alone with a class of 36 hyperactive kids. My time in South Africa taught me a thing or two about improvising sports sessions, so it went better than expected. I kept it simple, and the kids just seemed to be happy to be outside with the novelty of having a new foreign teacher ordering them around.

I had also turned up to classes that were rearranged or even wholly cancelled without being alerted throughout the days. I was warned this would happen due to the relationships within hierarchies here, so I took it all in my stride with my feathers unruffled. Those higher up in the pecking order had minimal regard for those further down, meaning they would throw demands down the hierarchical ladder and expect them to be met without complaint. Occasionally, my lessons would be collateral damage, as with most, if not all, English Teachers in China. It would be nice to have some clarity, though.

Besides the senior staff treating my schedule like a Rubix Cube, the classes were fun and insightful. I found it helpful to keep introductory English lessons simple so I could gauge the quality of their language skills, therefore giving me the ability to plan accordingly for the classes ahead. I looked forward to progressing with them.

We also celebrated Teacher's Day. We, the foreign teachers, were treated to some milk tea and given a pomegranate to take home (A lack of sharp utensils and urgency caused mine to go stale). As grateful as I was, I still fell victim to a hint of envy when I saw some of my UK friends in other schools treated to bouquets, financial bonuses and boxes of chocolates to name a few of many gifts that outshone mine.

However, we did get the afternoon off for a Teachers' Day ceremony, where teachers and students performed dances, and singing and theatrical displays.

The ILP teachers were rehearsing for yet another dancing display and managed to rope me into taking part. Cathy bribed me with a milk tea to rehearse with them. I thought I would down my milky treat and see where it went. I reached my limit after 10 minutes of clicking my fingers and galloping on an imaginary horse along with some other actions that I've since deleted from my memory to save myself the trauma. I snuck out of rehearsal to find that Brennan had followed me out the door to chase me down. Brennan was a blonde, short, but a broad-shouldered man who was pretty athletic due to his wrestling background. When I saw he had hit a full sprint, I decided to accelerate myself and managed to lengthen the distance between us while laughing. He shouted from a distance "Come on, man, it's for the kids." This guilt-tripped me into trudging back, begrudgingly, and trying to muster up whatever it was I needed to go through with it. Whatever I tried to muster up did not last very long. I headed for the exit again less than 5 minutes later. I just could not bring myself to do it.

So opposed to preparing for the show, I was in the crowd, watching the show, sitting next to Anthony, who also refused to partake in the dancing. I said I felt a little bad because all of the other teachers were performing something. He laughed and responded, "I don't care! I ain't going out like that!" This made me feel much better. We were on the same page, and at least I tried. After watching their performance, I think we made the right decision. The Teachers' Day show concluded, along with our duties as teachers for the week. The bank holiday was upon us. Now I had a trip to Shanghai to orchestrate.

In retrospect, I find it insane how this opening week in Changzhou set a precedent for how my year living there would be. The impromptu introductions to people and experiences with people I had just met. The rather pivotal announcements that would be revealed in a remarkably understated manner. The insanely poor communication channels. The showcases, and the general way of life. At the time I thought things were up in the air because we were just settling in and they were adjusting to us. Little did I know, all the adjusting had to be done on my end.

Weekend in Shanghai

A day and a half of my teaching career had brought me to my first Chinese national holiday. It was a 3-day holiday to celebrate China's "victory" over Japan in World War 2. A narrative that my North American buddies and anyone who had any knowledge of World War 2 rightfully raised an eyebrow at. It was an event of great importance, and partially responsible for my stay in Beijing being so enjoyable. It was why the skies were a clear blue, you could take deep breaths without consequence, and you could see stars at night. In preparation for this momentous occasion and the celebration of the country's military might that would ensue, Beijing implemented several temporary regulations to reduce pollution. Factories were closed down, and traffic regulations were put in place by the Chinese Government. They had a system where only vehicles with odd/even numbers on their number plates could drive on each given day of the week, lowering congestion and consequently carbon emissions. There would be plenty of media coverage, so the skies had to be blue and the air smogless. Evidently, their citizens' everyday health and well-being were not a big enough priority to enforce any permanent changes of this nature.

I planned on using this holiday to reunite with my friends from the teacher training and visit Shanghai. I was planning to meet up with my old teaching partner Golnaz as well as Tom, who also lived in Suzhou. We had tried to orchestrate getting on the same train into Shanghai, as Suzhou station was the next stop from Changzhou. This couldn't happen because of limited train tickets so we decided I should meet them there.

I reached Shanghai, and the games began. I told them when I was arriving at Shanghai Station and assumed they would wait for me there. My first mistake was that this assumption was never communicated. I reached the Station, which was huge, and tried to get hold of Tom. We were both manoeuvring in and out of Wi-Fi friendly zones, as we were both yet to sort our phone contracts. It took me a good 35-40 minutes to find a place with a decent connection. I end up camped outside a KFC while trying to get hold of Tom and sustain a proper conversation. I managed to find out they were on East Nanjing Road, assuming if I hopped in a cab and told them this location, I would find them just like that.

I flagged down a cabbie, who thankfully spoke English. I told him where I needed to go. I reached my destination after about 5 minutes and was charged approximately 150 Yuan (£15). This took me aback, as I would be sceptical of being charged this in Central London at peak times and Chinese cabs were meant to be cheaper. I realised he didn't put the meter on and printed out receipts in Mandarin. I was already stressed from my quest for Wi-Fi, so I just sighed and gave him what he wanted. Better to learn this lesson now. I had a year's worth of cabbie etiquette to use these lessons for.

Stepping out of the cab, I realised Nanjing Road (Nanjing Lu in Chinese) would be the single biggest and most populated high street I had ever seen. Post research had proved that the road is no less than 5.5 kilometres and attracts approximately 1 million visitors daily. The magnitude of the task I had at hand was sinking in, and I was not very optimistic. The plus side was the group consisting of Tom, who was a 6'2, ginger-haired and rather muscular man, as well as a blonde-haired Grace, a brunette Sally, Sabrina, who was of Indian heritage and Golnaz, who was of Iranian origin. Golnaz was also pretty tall compared to the average resident, standing at roughly 5'8. I was hoping this group of diverse looking people would stand out to me amongst the ocean of Chinese shoppers.

However, we were on the high street with a ridiculous amount of shops, so I could easily walk past a shop they were inside of while trudging along the road. I walked relatively slowly because of a mixture of fatigue, not wanting to miss them and trying to take in the scenery. It was quite a spectacle. An incredibly long and broad road, with high street brands neighbouring each other the whole way through. There were also stalls in the middle of the road and people approaching you trying to sell you stuff. I did not get as many members of the general public ogling me, as foreigners are more common in Shanghai. People were also more concerned with navigating through the thick crowd of shoppers. When I did get a prolonged look, it was usually younger-looking women who liked what they saw. Their interest was more salacious rather than curious. It was a pleasant change to be stared at due to physical attraction instead of being a novelty. Objectification never felt so good.

To my relief, I managed to spot a fed-up looking Tom outside of a giant New Look and realised he was alongside Sabrina, who saw the look of exhaustion and stress on my face. She embraced me while I all but collapsed in her arms. They were both astonished that I had defied the odds to find them, and I was just happy the struggle was over. I asked Tom if he was all right, to which he replied that he had reached his limit for following around a group of 4 women while they shopped for clothes. I had started to think I may have been the luckier out of the two of us!

I waited with them at the door for a while before Grace and Sally re-emerged with shopping bags in their hands. I said my hellos and they would declare their shopping spree over. I timed my arrival to perfection. We made our way to the Metro station to find Theo waiting for our arrival. Grace and Sally lived near Theo, so we were all on the same train. Tom and I were going to stay with Theo and Golnaz with Grace and Sally. Sabrina headed home alone.

Theo had a pretty nice setup. His flat was in quite a swanky building. In the lift up to Theo's place, we shared the ride with one of the other residents who took a shine to us. He asked us where we were from in Mandarin. Luckily, Theo had studied some Mandarin before arriving in China, otherwise Tom, and I would have been clueless. Theo replied "Inguo ren" which is English in Mandarin. He then pointed at me and made his confusion known when we said I was also English. It seemed I did not fit the ethnic criteria of the English people he'd seen on TV, which probably consisted of The Queen, Mary Poppins and maybe David Beckham, if he was by chance a pop-culture enthusiast.

We had a few hours of much-needed downtime, talking about our first experiences of our respective cities and schools we were working in. Theo showed us some of his music, and we spoke about our stories leading up to this point and where we were hoping to go from that moment. We did not have a genuine chance of getting to know each other's backgrounds in Teachers' Training. We were either frantically throwing together lesson plans or doing some type of group activity, so intimate conversations were a rarity in small groups. This was a welcome change.

It was soon time to get ourselves ready. Theo put on some Rock and Roll music (more Chuck Berry than Red Hot Chilli Peppers), while we prepared ourselves and gave Tom a hard time about his light blue jeans and black polo t-shirt combo, which he took a bit to heart. Bless him.

We went to the restaurant first. The Chinese dining experience was a lot more communal. Rather than ordering a plate for yourself, you ordered multiple dishes and put them in the centre of the table, before taking a bit of everything for your plate. For me, I felt this element made group meals more intimate and enjoyable, giving you a chance to connect directly over the shared dinner as well as the conversation. My dining experiences in South Africa also had a similar dynamic.

Once we finished our meal, we headed to a bar, played a few drinking games and enjoyed each other's company. We followed that up by going to another bar Theo was familiar with. He talked about it as if it was the best place he had ever been to but on arrival the only people there were the staff. We made ourselves at home and enjoyed being the sole occupants before calling it a night and heading home.

The next day came around, and we had a pretty chilled one. Theo, Tom and I started the day with a makeshift treat for the tastebuds that we called our breakfast. We came across a bakery on our stroll down the street and decided to make a breakfast sandwich out of one of their pastries and some meat from one of the street food stands. We enjoyed our food from the comfort of a street corner's pavement where we sat and ate practically undisturbed, marvelling at our lively, unfamiliar surroundings, allowing a delicate balance of serenity and excitement to embrace our being. The roads were wide. Wide enough to fit four rows of traffic on either side, which was standard here. The sounds of differing vehicles formed a somewhat hectic instrumental to the surrounding area. Cars, trucks, vans, tuck tucks, e-bikes, you name it. The human traffic and undistinguishable chatter also graced my senses.

I realised how I was destined to spend the majority of this trip oblivious to what people are saying around me, regardless of how many people were speaking at the same time. I had not ventured too far without supervision up to this point. Now I was in Shanghai with two mates, left to our own devices. No guide, no translator, nothing. It was the feeling I came all this way for. To be outside of my comfort zone, experiencing something new every day. I was excited. I was ready.

After eating, we spent the day slowly wandering around in the summer heat, exploring shops as Theo needed to get a few small pieces of furniture for his apartment. We also needed to stock up on alcohol so that we could have a few pre-drinks before our night out. We bought a case of beer and split the expense between us, which set us up for the night.

We met with the other members of our group at different Metro stations on the way to our destination, a night club called Chemistry in the city centre. There was a group of at least 15 of us by the time we arrived. Grace managed to get connected with someone who could provide us with a table, as well as unlimited free alcohol for the night. We got the full VIP treatment because we were Westerners. From what I gleaned, having westerners in your club in China gave the place an image of modernity and made it look like a cool place to be.

Although I made the most of this opportunity, I knew for a fact I would be treated entirely differently if I arrived with a group of "westerners" who shared my complexion. But I was in party mode. Those thoughts could wait for another time, such as when I decided to write a book on my thoughts and experiences.

We enjoyed the novelty of having drinks all night for being foreign. I guzzled all the champagne and vodka I could get my hands on while kicking back in the VIP area. They played mostly techno music, which isn't my thing at all, so I didn't dance much. I went off to explore the club a few times, but other than that, I stayed in our area and just spoke to people in our group. However, a random wave of sadness overwhelmed me when I realised I wasn't going to see my youngest brother Josh for nearly a year. He was only four years of age, and I realised how much of his development I would miss. I don't know why he popped into my head at such a random time, but he did. Whether it was the alcohol or not, I don't know. But the thought got to me, and I felt like crying. I went to the toilet and sat in the cubicle so I could wallow in my drunken emotions uninterrupted. Ten minutes later, I reappeared with my composure regained, ready to enjoy myself again, being greeted by my mate outside the toilet door who happily let me know he had just pulled the girl I'd been talking him up to all night. I gave him a congratulatory hug, and we both headed back for the VIP area. As a faithful man in a relationship, I was more than happy to provide the assist.

On our way out the club, we realised one of our group members had over-indulged in the free festivities and was losing her fight with consciousness. A few of us attempted to sober her up as a cab was waiting for her, but she could barely stand up. Her failure to maintain eye contact with me for over 2 seconds made it clear she would never make it to that cab alone. I took it upon myself to pick her up and carry her to the taxi. She hugged me and kissed me on the cheek as a token of her gratitude while I walked up the road in the rain with her in my arms. Theo later compared it to a scene from Hercules, which was quite funny.

The level of alcohol consumption got the better of me on my cab ride home, and I fell asleep. Theo and Adam were discussing getting something to eat. It was a great idea, but I had to come to terms with my night being over. I could barely keep my eyes open, and I don't think any food I'd consume in that condition would have stayed down. I took Theo's key and made my way to his flat, leaving the two of them to find a meal. By the time they got back, I was out cold.

The morning came, and it was time to make my way back to Changzhou. Tom and I met with Golnaz, and we made our way to the Metro station. We spent the journey to Shanghai Station drifting in and out of sleep, recovering from the night before. I enjoyed two fun nights there, which consisted of great food from restaurants and street vendors alike. There was a lot of alcohol consumed at minimal, if not zero, cost and I spent it among good company. I had every intention of meeting with Theo and Tom again to enjoy more of what Shanghai had to offer (it never materialised). Until then, it was back to reality.

Being Big and Black in China

Upon arrival back in Beijing, I could not help but notice that among the influx of foreign teachers ready to exert our Englishness amongst the population, I happened to be the only Black person, making me the sorest of the sore thumbs. During the orientation day, I had become friends with Nicole. We hit it off straight away, and I was looking forward to reuniting with her out here, shared blackness aside. To my joy, she arrived later in the training camp. But I digress.

Moreover, my complexion is dark, and I stand at a towering height of 6'4 with an athletic build, which would render me quite the specimen in observation for most people, let alone the Chinese. This had put me in a unique situation, as the majority of foreign students could find refuge in a bubble of white Britishness. The friendships I forged within it would not change the fact I would still be "The Black Guy".

Although the prior warnings were accurate, there was not much said on possible differing experiences based on individuals' racial backgrounds. From my time in China, I believed my ethnicity had contributed to me being perceived differently from other "Western" immigrants, and I hope to give an insight on exactly why.

This was exemplified by the moment I was asked by two of my colleagues if they could feel the texture of my hair. I had no problem with this as they were friends and had the decency to ask, but it was a perfect example of my racial solitude amongst the nationally united. Being born in the same country and sharing a language made my anatomy no less of a source of curiosity. A curiosity my colleagues had the luxury of being relieved of within the group. I was still "othered" by the group of people in this country I was meant to feel closest to and most integrated with.

Before breaking away from our British haven and into the streets of Beijing, I recall having a conversation with my roommate Daniel, about which one of us would garner the most attention amongst the locals. Honestly, I was surprised this was even questioned and made it clear I thought I would be the obvious choice. After a short discussion, we agreed to let time settle the debate, which did not take long. After 10 minutes of roaming the streets by my side, he compared walking with me to "having a really hot girlfriend that everyone keeps staring at" due to the number of people who had their eyes glued to me as we walked past. This was a pretty common trend. Other ventures with teachers into Chinese terrain have inspired comments such as "I feel like just another citizen again when I walk with you" or "I like coming out with you because you take the heat off me". I had been nicknamed "The Celeb" by some friends due to the heightened attention I received and how often it was shown through photograph requests.

However, I am no stranger to eyes being drawn to me out of curiosity. My aforementioned physique means there are very few places I can thoroughly blend in due to my size alone. There was also the fact that although my hometown in the London metropolis boasts an incredibly diverse pool of ethnicities, the UK as a whole is less than 3% Black. With that said, I have to come to terms with the fact I would be a rare "in the flesh" sighting for many people once I step outside of the UK's more diverse areas. Their reactions to me are much less extreme, but the principle was still the same. With these experiences under my belt, I have managed to develop defence mechanisms to deal with the racially induced spotlight I had to endure in China. I believe this, along with my generally composed nature had helped me handle the unwanted attention.

When relocating to another nation where the people look nothing like you and cultural practices are incredibly different to yours, the foreign alien can usually take solace in strongly identifying with their homeland. The place you are born and raised in will play a significant role in the person you become, whether you like it or not. The language you speak, your choice of colloquialisms, taste in entertainment, social habits, and the list goes on, delving into practically every fabric of your identity. With that being said, you are never more aware of how much the place you call home has moulded you until you are removed from it. Until you end up in a place where you do not have to be as detailed when analysing the subtle physical and behavioural differences between you and others to identify what makes you unique. Through the haze of estrangement, you find clarity in knowing who you are and what you represent.

However, I have been met with much incredulity when announcing my nationality, with numerous times being met with the response,

"English? But you're so Black?" or an inquisitive look that my white colleagues do not receive when stating the same fact. The fact that I was speaking and teaching the language of the nation was not enough to convince people I was born and raised there. Honestly, I have never been the biggest patriot, and with Britain's past and present relationship with racism/colonialism I never will be. Regardless, being completely dissociated from Britain was always going to be disorienting.

Moreover, my blackness itself has come into question. While teaching my classes, I've had many students attempt to touch me or stroke my skin just to see how it feels. Which didn't take me aback until I spotted one child run his finger down my arm and check if any of my blackness had rubbed off onto his tip. He proceeded to make a confused face at the discovery of his finger not being blackened and still found it necessary to brush his finger off onto his shirt while looking disgusted.

In the context of the national culture, this action begins to make more sense. When you take into consideration how much skincare/shower/cosmetic products use skin bleaching agents here, you can see that for every association of beauty and cleanliness they have is for lighter skin; the opposite would apply for darker skin. There was an advert released during China that spurred global scrutiny. The scene was a Black man trying to kiss a Chinese woman while wearing dirty clothes and having paint on his skin. The woman avoided the kiss and went on to push the man into the washing machine. Once the cycle was finished, the man rose from the washing machine with not only clean clothes, but he became Chinese! A prime example of blackness being seen as literally dirty in Chinese culture.

Those factors combined have left my mind in a frenzy of questions regarding what Chinese people see when my large black frame dominates their glance. What do I represent to them? What stereotypes do they have about black people and how many do I adhere to?

It caused me to feel lost and uncertain as these questions fly around my head, as the answers would remain elusive. With a population as vast as China's with provincial and social class cultures varying to such a high degree, the answers would also change to a considerable extent depending on the individual.

These events had made me question whether the interpretation of "celebrity status" had oversimplified the notion of the excessive attention received here. My experiences have shown there are more dimensions to this concept than being overwhelmed by seeing a non-Chinese person walk amongst them. I also feel that many past accounts of foreign experiences in China have been relatively one-dimensional. It could be due to the lack of diversity in writers willing to touch on the topic or the lack of "Black Westerners" who have been to China, or both.

With that said, I feel perspective plays a huge role. The average white person in their lifetime is rarely subjected to negative discrimination due to race. If their race is highlighted, the reason is usually positive. This may cause a white person to misinterpret or glamourise their racial profiling as they are used to it being for a good reason.

Whereas the majority, if not all, Black Westerners have been subjected to more negative treatment in terms of racial discrimination. There are more negative stereotypes and perceptions of Black people than any other race, so when our ethnicity is highlighted, it would be understandable if one of us would be more scrutinising of why that is the case. Not to say other Westerners of colour would not have the same mentality, they probably do, but I am specifically talking about the Black experience now, as it is my own.

Through those experiences, I saw somewhat of an opportunity through their ignorance. These events were simply a result of an absence of genuine experiences with people from my ethnic background. Upon realising this, I became aware that I was in a position to be a trailblazer of sorts. For many people here, I would be the very first Black person they would have a meaningful interaction with, so I was in a position to set the precedent for those who would come after me. It was a balancing act, as I wanted to leave people with a good impression of my people, but I also needed to draw a line in terms of what was appropriate for them to do or say to me. To us. It could be seen as a lot of pressure to some, and it is definitely not fair that any one person's actions should bear the scrutiny of their whole race, but that was the reality of the situation. I found it different from the notion of being a token/acceptable black person back in the UK. Those situations, although just as unfair, are people trying to divert from the preconceived stereotypes they may have of Black people and diluting yourself to assimilate to what other races may deem as appropriate or acceptable. In China, I was working with a completely clean slate. I was laying the foundations, not conforming to foundations laid by others to avoid judgement, which I would never approve of as much as I understand it.

Either way, I felt I would be doing a grave disservice to the potential Black voyagers looking for further insight on what they might experience during their time in China if I didn't write this. China is an enormous country with cultures and mentalities differing from province to province, so your experience may be completely different depending on your visit, but I still hope what I've written somewhat braces you for what you may be heading into.

The Swing of Things

My return from Shanghai heralded the end of my leisurely existence in China. I was about to start a full term of teaching. I began etching out what would soon become a daily routine and imprint myself into the school as hopefully, a valued member of staff. The euphoria was starting to fade, and reality was beginning to creep back into the frame. I had a job to do.

On the day of my first coaching session, I woke up at 6 am to prepare myself for what laid ahead. Luckily my commute was a one-minute walk, as I lived on campus. I walked out into the playground and saw it buzzing with life. I saw kids on the track training for athletics, kids in formation practising Kung Fu, and a myriad of other exercises. I think it was the most lively I had ever seen a school facility at 6.30 am. I felt like I was the new kid in one of those American High School movies, walking through different crowds and cliques, taking in my new and lively surroundings while trying to figure out where I fit in.

I saw a group of boys and one girl, with the majority of them dressed appropriately for football and guessed it would be my group. I introduced myself to the children before nervously checking my watch. The head coach was yet to arrive, and the training time was fast approaching. I hoped Cathy didn't stitch me up again like with my P.E lessons the week before. I was grossly unprepared to take this session alone.

To my relief, I spotted John walking towards us. When I first met him, he spoke of his excitement of working with me. I looked forward to seeing how football translated to children here and how his coaching style may differ with mine.

John led the session while I stepped in now and then to give individual players more attention when necessary. I stopped them when I saw their technique could be corrected or improved with some wise words or a demonstration. The highlight of the session for me was when I pulled the girl aside. I showed her how to shoot with her laces, to then witness her bury her next effort into the bottom corner. I grinned with pride and congratulated her on her return. Go on, girl!

John then split the group into two and asked me to oversee one of them. I did just that. We were doing a simple passing drill. Once I saw the kids had grasped it well, I used my initiative and gave them more complex conditions to progress the exercise. I wanted to keep it challenging for them. As soon as John heard me giving new instructions, he rushed over to me while saying "no no no no no". Once he got within talking distance of me, he pointed to his clipboard and said, "My plan!". I nodded and carried on with what he asked—my first run-in with the Chinese hierarchy's rigid nature. I have worked under football coaches in the UK multiple times. Adding your ideas to coaching drills was always welcomed and to a degree, expected, as long as they were good and cohesive with the drill's objective.

After the session ended, John pulled me aside and said he would let me run tomorrow's session, which I looked forward to.

Once the sessions were over, I realised how strenuous these kid's schedules were. They were up playing sports at around 6:30 every morning before they even had a chance to eat breakfast. They'd then have a full day's school, and many children even had classes in the evening, continuing until up to 7 pm. What a long day!

The next morning arrived, and I was in full control of the session; for the best part of fifteen minutes anyway. Midway through one of my passing drills, John must have got bored with playing second fiddle, as he decided to take full control. I had a feeling this was an early indicator of how much coaching I would get to do. I just hoped the quality of his coaching proved to be good enough to maintain my enthusiasm as an understudy. As long as I was working under someone I could learn from, it was fine by me.

In terms of teaching, I was pretty happy with the setup, to begin with. I was teaching 15 classes a week, with the three morning football sessions. For my first English session, I pretty much based it around the basics of British culture, such as the sports we like, the tourist attractions and other things widely associated with the UK. I made a conscious effort to incorporate pictures showing the diverse nature of the UK. Adults and children alike had shown me confusion whenever I said I was English because they did not associate the nationality with

Black skin. I thought it would be a perfect way to get them used to the idea of the UK being diverse. Anthony never had that issue. China's love for basketball had acquainted them with the darker-skinned population of America.

One lesson I walked into was a grade 2 class. I realised I would have to simplify my plans. Little did I know how much. The majority of Chinese people who speak English have an English name and a Chinese one, as they know how hopeless most English speakers would be in pronouncing, writing and remembering their names. I turned up to find out none of those children had their English names yet. This meant for the whole lesson I turned into a human name generator. I picked kids one by one and gave them whatever name popped into my head. The kids loved it, and I had fun but could not help but feel like I was getting away with murder. I was thinking up names and dishing them out at random. Somehow this passed as teaching. I guess they were learning names. I realised afterwards that I was actually in the wrong classroom. This made sense, as it would not have been logical to leave a class so new to the language in my hands. What did surprise me was the teacher in the room stepped aside and let me do my thing without argument. I thought she was my assistant! Either way, she was a great help.

The P.E sessions were straightforward. I had taught P.E at primary schools before, so I just carried out similar drills but to a larger class. Much larger. I always had at least one other coach partnering me, and we would split a class of 30 in half. This time I had 40+ kids to myself. I tried and failed to play more intricate games with the children. The language barrier became more apparent the more I tried to break down rules. Consequently, I kept it to basic exercises and cranked up the difficulty as lessons progressed.

My English classes were near perfect in terms of behaviour. The lessons went as smoothly as I could have imagined, and their enthusiasm never boiled over. However, in my P.E. classes, I had very mixed experiences in terms of their behaviour. They have varied from a class of model students to me having to make the entire classes sit down for short intervals, due to them being out of control. With one class, I even resorted to making them run punishment laps. This was not usually how I asserted my authority with children I worked with, but they had a way of bringing out my inner disciplinarian. I felt bad when after their laps, kids would start coughing. Only then it sunk in exactly how bad the pollution was. I still had no plans to tolerate their sass.

I found that children in classrooms are much easier to maintain order with. After such a strenuous schedule, the chance to stretch their legs outside can prove to render them over excitable. As much as I sympathised with them, leniency does not get you very far, and I had to do my job correctly, which included keeping these kids in line.

There was a standout moment where I failed miserably in disciplining one of my students. I was going to single out a girl in the 4th grade for a telling off before she threw me off.

'Teacher, your eyes!' she exclaimed.

'What about them?' I responded impatiently.

'They're so beautiful!' she responded enthusiastically.

I was completely disarmed by the unexpected compliment and forgot why I was even angry. I thanked her and continued with the class, watching over their behaviour with my beautiful eyes.

The night market became the lifeblood of my evening meals. I was there practically every night. I fell into the routine of getting the same meal — a chicken wrap/kebab thing and a barbecue chicken portion from another stall. I'd also get a side of either rice or noodles depending on my mood. All for 25RMB (£2.50). Can't complain at all.

I became increasingly reliant on the night market as the consistency of the school dinner's quality varied day in and day out. I attended school meals, mostly to socialise with the other teachers. Even when the dinners were good, I would often find myself hungry again deeper into the evenings. We also could not cook for ourselves, as we had no access to a kitchen. I had a fridge/freezer and a microwave in my room as well as hot water from the dispenser. My choices were limited to reheating night market food and instant noodles. The quality of instant noodles in China was ridiculously good by the way. You could probably get away with serving it in some restaurants in the UK!

Consequently, my supermarket trips would mostly consist of buying snacks, drinks, noodles and fruit.

One evening, I went to the night market with Anthony and his friend, Michelle, who was also an American teacher who came through the same agency as Anthony. She was teaching in Changzhou too. While we were queuing for noodles, she found her long, flowing braids in the hands of a pair of old women who could not help themselves. This took me aback. As much attention as I had gotten during my time here, I had never been touched against my will. Anthony was laughing in hysterics. I asked her if I should step in, but she said it was fine. She genuinely didn't mind. I thought I would give them a taste of their own medicine and started fondling the hair of one of the women doing the same to Michelle. She turned around and laughed before enjoying Michelle's hair for a few more seconds. She then carried on with her evening. I don't think she got the message, but I guessed there was no harm done and carried on with ordering my food.

I spent one of my Fridays with a group of the ILP teachers to take a trip to a place they dubbed "Muslim Noodles". The place had Arabic on the shop sign as the owners originated from a province known for its Muslim population, Xinjiang.

The noodle place was ok. In all honesty, it was not that much better than the instant noodles I had from the supermarket. It did, however, give me an excellent chance to get to know the group better. I sat with Heidi and Devin, whom I sat with at my first meal with Changzhou. Devin was pretty surprised with how much I knew about the States. Not that I'm an expert, he just really underestimated the cultural impact the States had in the UK. I was somewhat surprised when the topic of 9/11 came up.

'Did you hear about the terrorist attack in New York years ago?' Devin asked. 'Two buildings were knocked down when a plane crashed into them.'

I looked at him in disgust and asked, 'Are you really breaking down 9/11 to me?' before laughing in disbelief.

Heidi spoke to me about her love for literature and said she was currently reading Zadie Smith, who is one of my favourites too. She was also an aspiring (now published) author, who spent much of her time in China writing a novel in between teaching or being a tourist.

On the walk back, while enjoying the amazing tastes of Coco's milk tea, I spoke to Heidi and Devin some more and confirmed Anthony's suspicions that the whole group (bar one) were, in fact, Mormons. We had talked about them before, and I realised none of them ever swore or even hinted at indulging in any alcohol consumption. This was always going to raise suspicions, considering the price of alcohol here and the size of the group. Anthony told me that Utah, the place where most of the group resided, was the Mormon capital in the US. I realised that I was in quite a unique position as I had never met a Mormon before and had only heard rumours about their practices of incest and multiple spouses. Now I could separate the fact from fiction.

They were well aware of the reputation they had outside of their community and even asked me if I had heard crazy stories about them having horns. I can confirm that Mormons do not encourage incest whatsoever, nor do they have horns. They broke down their fundamental beliefs, and as far as religion goes, it's not that crazy to me. I am an agnostic who was raised Catholic, so I would like to think I am balanced enough to give a fair opinion in terms of understanding the religious perspective without being swayed by bias.

Midway through my second week, I realised there might have been a misunderstanding with my schedule. I was turning up to the classes I was expecting to teach English, and the children were lining up outside of their classrooms, which was what they did before they had a P.E. lesson. I also remembered earlier in the week before I would teach an English lesson, the teacher passing the class onto me would ask me if I was taking them to P.E. class. I approached Cathy about my P.E.: English lesson ratio in one of my free periods. I was hit with the bombshell that my schedule had ZERO English classes! I had done my TEFL course with the help of a company called Teach English in China yet had no English lessons to teach. I was, and probably still am, the only teacher in their history to not be hired to teach English. It dawned on me that all the English classes I had taught were scheduled for P.E., and I was teaching rogue for nearly two weeks. My schedule was mostly Mandarin so I kind of guessed my way around which classes were P.E. and which ones were English.

This was a significant issue for me. I had taught P.E. before in the UK, but I left that role because I was bored with it. I did not come here to work at the same job I got bored with back home. The only difference was, the kids here were worse behaved, and there was a language barrier that restricted the activities I could do. I relished the challenge of teaching English since before the journey began, so I was not going to back down. I reminded them that my contract clearly states I would be a P.E. and English teacher, which I realised they probably only put on there to appease me enough to sign the dotted line. Cathy's defence was, she approached my agency asking for a P.E. teacher. However, I had spoken to her via email before anything was agreed and she said I would have English classes too.

The contract also said that the failure of either party to honour the agreement could result in a compensation package of 10,000RMB (£1000) for the affected party and the termination of the contract. I let them know I would trigger this if I had to and find another job elsewhere. I had a bit of a network here now. I was confident I could do so. I could have asked my friends in Suzhou to put in a word for me at their schools, and I also had friends in Nanjing through my lady, who was very well connected to schools and universities out there. I had already met with those who would become her supervisors in China while still in the UK. She thought it would be a good idea for me to meet them as our paths were going to cross sooner or later, so I accompanied her to her briefing.

I started looking forward to potentially moving to Nanjing as it was a lovely city, and I would be closer to my girlfriend. I would have happily taken my compensation package and moved on from Changzhou if they didn't meet my demands.

Bad scheduling aside, I had been treated pretty well. Cathy took Anthony and me to a meal along with some of the other Chinese staff one evening. I was pleased to be presented with a lovely steak dinner. It was a welcome change to the canteen meals, which can vary from the feast of your dreams to morale shattering disappointment. I made the most of her generosity and ordered a second plate of food after demolishing the first plate. Cathy used that time to express her fondness of both of us and said she planned to treat us to a trip to the cinema when she decided to take us next (That never happened). She also said that she hoped our stay extended to another year (That never happened either, Anthony stayed on though). After the meal, they went back to campus.

I thought we were going to get a lift home as we were still very new to the city, but it was not meant to be. Not that I was any less grateful for the outing. I had no idea where I was, but luckily for me, Anthony had explored this area before. He said he would know how to get us home as long as we found a Tesco that was meant to be nearby. We were unsuccessful in our search, but we walked by a basketball court in the middle of a shopping complex on our wander. It was quite a cool scene. Neon lights and shop windows surrounded a group of players shooting hoops. We were invited to join in and take some shots. After sinking a few, they asked if I could dunk for them. I gestured towards my jeans, showing they restricted my movement, rendering me incapable of showing off my abilities. I showed them a video Anthony had of me dunking so they knew I wasn't lying about my ability to do so.

Anthony and I had bonded a lot over basketball. I was not an avid fan like he was, but I played in school and still loved a swish. I also added dunking to my repertoire out here as I'd just mentioned. On our first time on the court in the school premises, I vowed to Anthony that I would learn to dunk before I left here. I managed to land one on my first attempt! We played one on one a few times as well as a few matches with/against the school's P.E. teachers. The teachers were outstanding. What they may have lacked in height, they made up for in every other department. They were worthy teammates and opponents.

Anthony was a good player. His handles were solid; he was quick and agile. My height advantage and sharpshooting were a bit much for him, but against others, we made a nearly unstoppable team. I know he will be reading this, so before he texts me death threats, I will admit how much better he is at chess than me. I thought I was a good player until I faced him on his prestigious chess set, with the pieces being hand-crafted Ancient Egyptian mini statues. He owned the most aesthetically pleasing chess set I had ever played on. We played over 20 times, and I only beat the guy once. One more time than he beat me on the court, though!

One welcome surprise in my chaotic scheduling was the school trip to the zoo. It was a rainy day, but it did not dampen our spirits. As well as being graced by the powerful and elegant presence of the white tiger, I saw red pandas, baby tigers at feeding time and a hippo fight! Not to mention I got framed snaps of myself holding a baby monkey and a lion cub. As lovely as some of those pictures were, I had mixed emotions when I realised how small the cages they were being kept in were. If I knew how bad the conditions were, I would have never gotten them done, and by the time I did, it was too late. That cub was insanely powerful. I struggled to hold it while it fought for freedom. I marvelled at the thought of how strong an adult lion must be.

There was also a circus show. There was a myriad of performers, humans and animals alike, even Black people. My mood soured when I realised the only Black performers were wearing leopard print rags and jungle sounds played as they performed their flips and tricks. I was disgusted. The first representation of Black people I had seen in the country was primitive jungle-dwelling back flippers. I was even more surprised that I seemed to be the only one to notice that this was a problem; either that or others felt too awkward to bring it up. I took an unorthodox approach of taking a nap for the show's remainder as a peaceful protest. I did not want to dignify this racist show with my attention, so when I felt myself yawning, I gave in to the wave of tiredness. Quite possibly the most peaceful protest in history.

There were also other displays of animal cruelty shown in other shows and exhibitions. The most disturbing for me was the bears on their hind legs walking around in costumes performing tricks. They looked so uncomfortable and unnatural; it left a bad taste in my mouth. This was a bit much for me to witness. Overall, it was a delightful day and a welcome break from regular school scheduling. It did put me off visiting zoos for life though. Let those animals go!

The highlight for me in this period had to be my girlfriend's arrival in China. She arrived a week before I got to see her, as she had to settle into Nanjing and become acquainted with her accommodation, uni campus, new dorm-mates and scheduling. Even though seeing her was delayed, it was lovely being in the same time zone as her. We could text and call each other throughout the day again as opposed to her trying to find time in the middle of the day while I was winding down for bed. Weekdays also felt like they were going quicker because I had a reunion with her to look forward to. I felt like it only made sense for me to head to Nanjing instead of her coming up to Changzhou. I was already settled into the place and had experience travelling on trains out here so it would be less stressful for me to make the trip.

When talking about the moment we'd reunite, I joked that we'd both drop our bags and embrace while being illuminated by a random Chinese sign placed above us. This became a self-fulfilling prophecy as we arranged to meet, and I called her name when I glimpsed her walking across the road. Although I had an inexplicably amazing time leading up to this moment, it felt like our adventure began here. The team was complete.

Our weekend was not an eventful one. We did not feel the need to do much as we were just happy to be in each other's company again. We strolled around the local area, ate at some local restaurants and took it easy. We had the rest of the year to make an adventure of my visits to Nanjing, so we did not feel any urge to exert ourselves. There was one memorable moment where we went to KFC. It was late, and most places were closed, leaving a limited choice in places to eat. We were both starving, so we ordered one of the family bucket meals. The woman on the cash register was acting star struck from the moment we arrived, staring dumbfounded with an imperishable smile while she fired questions at us regarding our heritage. We answered accordingly while the staff at the back prepared our food. She was so in awe of our presence that she bid us farewell without even charging us! On our way out, my girlfriend whispered, 'Did we pay for this?'

'Nope! Keep walking!' I replied, masking laughter while we slightly upped our pace towards the door. It was the sweetest tasting meal from the place I've ever tasted.

Golden Week

What we had as opposed to a half-term break was a national holiday called "Golden Week," which stemmed from the National Day of The People's Republic of China on October 1 and allowed us an extra three days off. I opted against using the week to explore other parts of the country as my near immediate start to teaching left me barely any time to get to know Changzhou. The ILP teachers mostly took the week off as an opportunity to travel across the country. They had a limited time in the country as well as the disposal of their parent's seemingly limitless bank accounts, which they seemed to be making the most of. I did not have that luxury, so I thought I would explore the local area a bit more.

On my first day, I did precisely that. I explored a local place resembling a temple, which I had passed a few times on the bus. It turned out to be a theme park/relic park/safari. I came across a park with a small football pitch and basketball court, where I was invited to shoot some hoops. A lovely dude who introduced himself as Derek saw me walk past and asked me to join in. We hit it off straight away. He was impressed with the fact that I came out here to teach, and I liked how he took pride in owning a business and being independent. He was in his mid-thirties and joked about his prime athletic years being behind him and how smoking probably didn't help his cause. We could only have so much chitchat. We had to play next.

I was utterly taken aback by how good they were and ended up having some of the most challenging matches since I had arrived. I managed to shake off my lax, leisurely stroll mentality and find my groove, to the joy of the spectators, who cheered from the sidelines. My shots started to come off, and my movement was sharp. We swapped WeChat's with the hope of linking up again soon to play. For some reason, his display picture was of a Caucasian child at the time, which was a bit weird to me. He never mentioned having a foreign wife or half/foreign child, which I would have guessed he would bring up, as I was also foreign. Our reunion never came to fruition, unfortunately. I was busy the next time he messaged me, and then the winter season made itself known and quelled all motivation for outdoor sports. By the time the weather warmed up he was buried among a sea of WeChat contacts I would see one time, with the hope of a future meet up that would never come to fruition.

After the game and a failed attempt to find my Ray-Bans after dropping them on my walk, I decided to check out a bar nearby I had walked past earlier. The pub logo was of a football on fire. I also peeped through the window for a closer look to be graced with the view of framed replica football shirts as well as a huge TV and a pool table. The place looked destined to become my second home.

A petite, middle-aged Chinese woman appeared at the door with a beaming smile, ushering me inside although the place was yet to open. She could not speak English, but she was intent on being the best host she could be. We started playing pool after she surprisingly offered to play me. The gesture was even more endearing as she was terrible! I thought about how appreciative I was of her partaking in an activity she was far from accustomed to just to appease me while I wiped the floor with her. Her hospitality was not in vain as the bar started to gain customers while she kept me occupied.

I met some middle-aged foreigners and got a few more challenging games of pool under my belt while enjoying some beer. I managed to catch some of the Premier League highlights playing on-screen while getting to know the owner of the bar. He was a German immigrant and an engineer by day. I found out he was one of quite a few Germans in China who found their engineering careers stagnating in their homeland, so moved here for more opportunities. He was also one of many white males out there who settled down with a younger, astonishing beautiful Chinese lady who would most likely be out of their league back in their homelands.

I thought I found my second home until they gave me my tab. £10 for 4 pints doesn't sound too bad initially, but when you know you could buy 12-15 pints for the same price from the supermarket or a non-western bar it becomes pretty steep! I began to feel guilty about voicing my intent to return there earlier that night, as I knew that was the last time they would ever see me.

My next venture around Changzhou was not as pleasant. I took a bus further into town and explored one of the many malls I had passed on my bus journeys. I approached one of the stalls in the centre of the market as I had taken an interest in their cologne options. Within seconds, I had sparked the attention of the shop floor assistant. What I thought was him greeting me with a smile was just him looking at me and laughing. I nodded as I came to terms with my status as a walking punchline and walked away. I was seriously considering making a purchase too, but not after their awful customer service.

I spent the rest of the day browsing around different clothes shops, trying to flush the image of that idiot's grin from my memory. I found this problematic as the attention I was receiving did not waver. It was not as blatantly disrespectful as the guy at the cologne stand. Still, that experience made it difficult for me to feel flattered by the pointed fingers and intrigued eyes in my direction.

Eventually, I grew bored and slightly agitated from exploring the mall and headed for the exit. I walked down the street towards the bus stop, passing three Chinese people behind the counter at a milk tea stand. 'Hello!' a girl shouted once I was around ten yards past the stand.

I turned around. I saw her smiling at me. She looked like she was in her late teens. Her two male colleagues looked about the same age.

'Come here!' she shouted again.

I was hesitant to engage with her as my experience at the mall had exhausted my patience. However, her ability to speak English made me think she may have sought a genuine conversation. I took a few steps towards her only for her to respond by ducking behind the counter while giggling. She had a playful look with a hint of fear, resembling a child playing with their parent or elder sibling who was pretending to be a monster.

'Are you f******* serious?' I muttered to myself while looking to the heavens.

I turned away in frustration, continuing my journey to the bus stop. I was trying to understand what just happened. Why would she duck underneath the table when I was already walking towards her? What was her end goal? Was she genuinely scared of me? Either way, the unwarranted disrespect I was on the receiving end of throughout the day had soured my mood. I had gotten used to the attention, but I felt the events today had a touch of malice I had not experienced before. What happened at the milk tea stand was the bitter icing on a disgusting cake. I just wanted to get myself indoors. Safe from prying eyes. Safe from scrutiny. Safe from ridicule.

I spent the rest of my holiday with my girlfriend, who came to visit from Nanjing. When she arrived, we explored more of the town, and I showed her around the few places I knew, as it was her first time in the City. We also visited the Tianning Temple, one of Changzhou's few tourist attractions. I found walking around with her considerably easier. As a unit, we both split the attention somewhat evenly. We were also often in our own bubble, indulging in conversations and enjoying each other's company. This acted as a welcome buffer between us and any unwanted attention.

We spent the last of our free days in Nanjing. We got a cab to where we thought our hotel was from the station. For the life of us, we could not find this place. We reserved our room online, so we were determined to find it. We marched up and down the same roads with our hefty luggage for a good 40 minutes before we decided to pay a premium rate for a room at a completely different hotel. The room was pretty standard, but I experienced for the first time, a hotel window that didn't lead outside! Weirdly, it was a window that led to someone else's room. I only opened it partly so we could maintain privacy, but I could smell their cigarette smoke seeping into our room. I decided to keep it closed. I could not recall ever being in a room with no natural light or access to fresh air, but I was too tired from travelling to dwell on those claustrophobic triggers and had a much-needed lie-down. I guess the concrete jungle that makes up most of China's inner cities was so densely populated, and the hotels were designed for stocking as many people as possible.

As we were in Nanjing, it became my girlfriend's turn to be the tour guide. She took me to the well-renowned Confucius Temple, which had the perfect scenery to round off what was a great week. We went on a boat ride that turned out to be quite a romantic setting. The lights illuminated the temples, shops, and surrounding buildings reflected into the water, causing the colours to rhythmically dance into each-other, decorating an already beautiful lake. It made an ideal location to allow the prior travel stresses to drift away. I could return to appreciating the fact I was cruising on a lake in China with the woman I loved, absorbing views from scenes worthy of the most lucidly creative imaginations. It was a breathtaking evening.

The next day we went to the Nanjing Gallery, which had some great paintings that moved me, namely Chen Zhifo's pieces. It spawned some artistic inspiration on my part for some lyrics and song ideas I still have written down somewhere. Unfortunately, that marked my last day in Nanjing and the end of Golden Week. It was back to Changzhou and back to not teaching English. Regarding my English lessons, thanks to some vigilant action from the Teach English In China team back in the UK, the process of finalising my English lessons would be in full swing once Cathy returned from Australia within a week. Anthony and I had also shortlisted some classes we were willing to swap with each other if it became a necessary option. With that said, I have been happily teaching P.E. with the knowledge of a solution being within touching distance.

The midweek placing of the holiday's end meant we had a short return to teaching before having a half-day of teaching on Saturday. I used this as an opportunity for an extended reunion with the Teachers staying in Suzhou. Tom, Mike, and Sam hosted a gathering in their house and were nice enough to let me sleepover. It was a pleasant atmosphere and one I had craved. The drinks flowed as freely as the conversation while music played in the background. Because all of the teachers in Changzhou were Mormons, I never experienced a setting of such a nature, although I enjoyed their company.

I had managed to catch up with everyone and hear their experiences of teaching in Suzhou. Everyone seemed over the moon with their journey so far. I met a Scottish dude who was struggling to handle his drink while the rest of us struggled to handle his awful taste in music. One song he selected that stuck out to me was a sonically horrifying heavy metal rendition of Jay-Z and Kanye West's N****s in Paris. I thought I was the only one suffering from his Spotify playlist, but as he later fell asleep upstairs, everyone began to ridicule how terrible it was. I took the responsibility as DJ and did my best to give a well-rounded crowd-pleasing performance, garnering praise from those who were complaining before. Mission accomplished. They lived right next to their very own mini-night market, which was a fantastic revelation to me. Heavy drinking brings to the forefront a large appetite for the majority of people, and I am no different. Sitting on tables outside with everyone and devouring our cheap fried treats was the perfect way to round off the night before everyone said their goodbyes and jumped into cabs home. I dozed off on the sofa with a full stomach, a light head and high spirits.

The morning called for more food. Tom and Mike had told me about a place down the road that served a dish called Garli Nuro. I don't know the translation, but when the plate arrived, I was treated to a large helping of beef and gravy mixed in with potatoes. It was a joy to behold. It sounds a very British meal, but they added their own spices to give it a unique flavour. The end-product was incredible. The mix of meat and heavy carbs was also a perfect way to soak up any excess alcohol in my system from the night before.

Next on the agenda was going shopping to get the necessary ingredients for dinner. I cycled through town with them using their other roommate's bike. It was a lovely cycle as Suzhou proved to be infinitely more scenic than Changzhou. Roads were often bordered by stretches of trees and greenery that arched over passing vehicles. It was a joy to pass through. As notorious as Chinese roads were for being the 2nd most dangerous in the world, they were great at ensuring cyclists and motorcyclists/e-bikers. Every road had a wide bike lane, and the conduct in those lanes was much more relaxed than the driving lanes where everyone was swerving around trying to beat the traffic by any means necessary. The sun was shining, the wind flowed through my hair, and we also got a lot of attention from the locals which we entertained. I occasionally shouted "NI HAO" if a crowd waved, which was often met by cheers and laughter. We were all smiles.

Tom and Mike served their signature dish of pork chops, mashed potatoes and vegetables, the touch of Britain I did not know I needed until I had it. With time escaping me and another week of teaching to prepare for, I headed back to Changzhou, considering the fact I could have been calling this place my home. It was a far more superior city, and I did have good friends there, but I also now had good friends in Changzhou and the privilege of experiencing both locations. I did want to experience as much as I could in this place. Living in Changzhou and being able to visit Suzhou at will gave me that luxury, as well as a larger social circle. Who was I to complain?

Back to English

Finally, I attended my first Kung-Fu lesson in China. One of the P.E. teachers was a skilled martial artist, and he was nice enough to put some time aside after school to teach us a thing or two. We learned some of the basic moves with the long sticks, and I got the hang of it pretty quickly. I planned to embrace the false feeling of invincibility whenever a snooker cue or detachable broom handle was in close proximity. I also learned how to do this spinning jump kick thing I can't quite describe but want to tell you about anyway. Unfortunately, I did not have many chances to expand on my skills, as the morning Kung-Fu lessons run at the same time as the school team's football training, which I help coach. I hoped to sort something out so I could add to my minimal set of moves.

I had managed to sort out my mattress situation too. A new English Teacher started working in our school and was staying in the room next to mine. What I didn't know was due to her back problems, she had requested a new mattress, and one was left outside for her in the hallway. Seeing a vacant king-sized mattress in the hallway on my return from teaching, I took a picture of it, sent it to Cathy and asked if I could have it. She responded with a yes, and I took it to my room and began disinfecting it as well as I could (the mattress was bare).

The new teacher revealed to me that the mattress was hers, and I felt awful. I told her Cathy said I could take it and did what any decent human being would do and insisted on giving it back, also letting her know it was disinfected and ready for use. She insisted that I keep it and said she would buy another one. I guess everybody wins. Finders keepers!

One problem that was beginning to arise for me was maintaining my hair. It was around three months into my China experience, and I had not seen a single place that looked like they would know what to do with my forming afro. My hairline had practically become non-existent, a jagged mess crawling across my forehead. Even before the trip, I didn't have the strongest of hairlines due to a string of terrible barber experiences, which made me even more cautious about allowing my hair into the wrong hands.

Anthony kindly offered up his services. He told me he cut his brother's hair quite regularly at home and that he'd maintained his hair since coming to China. I was pretty impressed with how well he'd done with himself, so I thought I'd take a leap of faith and cheat on my barber. We had been invited to quite a big wedding, and I didn't want to look homeless from the eyebrows up. It's funny how I had jumped on a plane to the other side of the world to live a completely new life for a year without a second thought, to find my most significant moment of fear and hesitation coming from a simple haircut.

I sat in front of the mirror in his bathroom and let him get to work. It started well. My hair was level, my waves were once again prominent, and my beard was in excellent shape. My shape up was not sharp, but it looked ok once my hair was shorter. Anthony asked if he should shape me up, and I made the mistake of saying yes and allowing him to turn my hairline into a train wreck. I jumped out of my seat with horror and leaned closer to the mirror to analyse the atrocity he had inflicted on my hairline, and I was lost for words. One side was shaped up pretty well, but the other side was a mess. Anthony managed to do a bit of damage limitation, but I was shell-shocked by what had just happened.

He was apologetic, and I thanked him for his effort, but wow. I was just happy I was in China because I wasn't in the company of anyone who knew about Black hair. If I walked around London with that shape-up, I would've been heckled on the street and potentially a viral sensation for all the wrong reasons. I sent a picture to a few friends of mine back home, and my brother and they were in hysterics. The standout responses being:

"You look like two different people from each side" - Lindsey (Big Brother)

"It looks like you switched barbers at half time" – Javon (Close friend)

My girlfriend came over later that night and reassured me it was not that bad and was seemingly happy my hair was restored to some kind of order. I made a mental note to give The Oscars a call in the morning and put her forward for a "Best Actress" nomination, as I was nearly convinced my hairline was not in critical condition. It was, however, nice to be put at ease. I was also reassured she was in love with my inner beauty as much as what was my handsome outer shell.

The wedding we were invited to was courtesy of Cathy. Her son's best friend was about to get married, and she was nice enough to add some of the foreign teachers to the guestlist. Immediately after entry, we were ushered around the bride and groom to take a group photo in typical foreigner's fashion. In most cases, it would feel awkward to turn up at a stranger's wedding and instantly become the main attraction, but here it was expected.

It was a wedding like no other I had seen. They put on quite the show. There were showings of pre-wedding recordings on a projector, the groom singing to the bride, a clown making balloon animals and throwing them in the crowd as well as a game show. Not to mention the bride managed to find the time to change into 4 or 5 different extravagant dresses within the ceremony. This garnered a few expensive ideas for what she was thinking could be for our wedding one day.

There was also an impressive spread of food on display and a healthy supply of alcohol on offer which I and the other non-Mormons exclusively as no religious obligations held us back.

Some of the ILP teachers had to prepare for a dance performance, which was their ticket into the wedding. This was not their first performance either. They had been taken to quite a few weddings and events as part of the entertainment. I found it interesting how far the novelty of having a foreign workforce was being exploited. I do not think many other cultures would welcome a group of foreign strangers that weren't professional dancers to dance at their events. For me, there was no event big enough for me to literally dance my way into, but luckily that was not something I had to worry about. To each their own, I guess.

To round off the day, the best man/wedding host threw stuffed animals into the crowd. To my grave disappointment, he did not throw the giant Pikachu in my direction, but the memories of a joyful ceremony along with the great food were comforting enough for me to leave on a high note. Chinese culture and spectacle do go hand in hand. They love to put on a show at any given opportunity.

However, there was a weird moment where someone speaking to me gestured to my girlfriend and said, 'This is beautiful!'

We were both visibly taken aback. 'This?!' I exclaimed.

'Sorry, I mean she!'

I laughed and said 'OK.' We'll chalk that one up to it being his second language.

Regarding my English lessons, I was given two. I sat in on Anthony's English classes to see what I was getting in for, and he did the same with me. Funnily enough, he sat in on my most uncontrollable classes, and he took them off me as he relished the challenge of whipping them into shape. I had given up on them. The only thing I could compare these classes to was how the Kindergarten class used to act in the cartoon show "Recess". Wild, untamed, full of energy with absolutely no respect for authority. Best of luck, Coach Carter.

Although I did want more than I received, I decided to opt for the sense of continuity I had craved since my arrival and settle with my current schedule. My first English session did not go as planned due to my external hard drive deciding to fail on me just as I was about to begin. It was far from ideal, but my improv skills and my assistant teacher helped me get by. I was able to get my hard drive working by my next lesson at the cost of losing ALL my data from reformatting it.

I lost all my movies, music, photos and teaching materials. I had a lot of free time on campus in-between classes, and my Internet connection was excruciatingly slow at times due to my VPN, so I had been more reliant than usual on my hard drive. It was a bitter pill to swallow.

But I digress. The kids had a blast, and I was reminded of how much I enjoy teaching English. It felt good to have the variation back in my schedule and to be doing what I came here to do. However, I was disappointed in the fact that I was teaching 2nd Grade children. This meant I would have to simplify my lessons more and no longer use my platform to subtly teach my kids the joys of racial diversity. Still, I was once again excited to do my job and looking forward to the days to come.

Real Friends

"How many of us? How many of us? How many jealous? Real friends, there's not many of us, we smile at each other, but how many honest?"

– Kanye West.

It's funny because the Kanye song these lyrics are from was released around the same time the cracks in what I thought were going to be lifelong friendships, were starting to become irreparable. I felt this entry was a grave necessity. I had also spoken to several friends who had moved abroad on their adventures and experienced similar situations to me.

People who opted towards living abroad, even if not permanently, usually do so to broaden their horizons or try to "find themselves"; a term I have always found nauseating. Either way, you look at it, a significant component of a lot of people's desire to live abroad or travel comes from seeking self-growth. What I would find out the hard way is that the same self-growth can become an old friendship's worst enemy, and eventually lead to its demise.

When I announced I was going to China with my girlfriend, I felt like I was on the receiving end of a lot of doubt and negativity. The most irritating question I kept getting was "What are you gonna do if you split up? China's a big place to be alone in." They asked me as if I was not aware of the country's size or that every relationship has the risk of ending.

I gave a legitimate and well-thought answer every time. "I'll have my own life set up there. I'll live in another city, so I won't bump into her. I'll have my own friends, a whole network of teachers not tied with her so IF we did split, it would be hard, like all breakups, but I would have the means to enjoy my time in China without her, as she would without me," and was met with accusations of delusion and irrationality. It was almost like they were hoping I would soil myself and pull the plug on the whole trip once they revealed this possibility. At the time I felt like they were trying to reflect their insecurities onto me, as I was optimistic about taking a risk they would not or could not do.

I had seen interviews and read books from successful individuals who had consistently expressed how you would always face backlash when deciding to meliorate yourself. I felt like it was becoming a reality for me.

The reality was I got more support and encouragement from friends outside of my immediate circle and even from loose acquaintances or strangers whom I dared to tell about my situation. It was then I realised there was more than just surface-level disagreements coming between us. These guys were like brothers to me, and I felt more warmth and excitement from people that barely knew me.

In the majority of group interactions, there was a feeling of disproportionate negative energy being directed towards me. I felt like I was walking on eggshells. From a spelling error in the group chat to any flaw in my statements I would get a flurry of comments opposing me, whereas when the shoe was on the other foot, nobody would be in my corner. It was a blatant shift I could see and feel, regardless of their efforts to play it down when I confronted them on the matter.

I must admit, there were many changes in me as a person, but I think they were all for the better. My knee injury prevented me from any exercise for the best part of 18 months and stopped me playing football for two years. Before this period, football was a massive part of my identity. Without it in my life for such a long time, I was forced to redefine myself. Well, either that or continue my ongoing descent into an ocean of self-pity and depression. I was transitioning from a footballer to a writer, eventually branching out to becoming a rapper. I was becoming more artistically inclined, more in tune with my emotions and waged war on ignorance, arming myself with an arsenal of books. I was becoming comfortable with who I was and the person I was growing into. I was having less frequent contact with the group. We went to different universities, started working full-time jobs, had relationships and were building our own lives. My changes were arguably the most extreme in the group. I think it was a shock to their systems. It felt like some of my friends were reluctant to warm to the perspective I was developing. Our differing views became more prominent and what used to be banter became personal attacks.

They could sense the distance between them and me growing and instead of analysing what they could be doing to cause the rifts they decided to blame it all on the one tangible variable outside of our group dynamic—my girlfriend. The narrative of "she's changed you," took centre stage. I think that became the narrative as it absolved them from taking any blame for their questionable actions. I laughed at this, as it could not have been further from the truth, and she warned me it would happen.

The mental gap between us became physical once I moved to China. The only means of maintaining communication between us was our infamous WhatsApp group. After a few back and forths, the inevitable actions of everyone jumping onto the side of whoever was against me, it resulted in me leaving what my primary means of communication with who were meant to be my closest friends was.

I was too far removed to entertain that situation. To them, it was just jokes and the nature of the group dynamic, despite me making it clear I was not a fan of this dynamic and I would not stick around much longer if it stayed the same. I was coming off the back of some of the best moments in my life in a new country, learning and growing with every passing day. Their messages were reminders of how stagnant the group as a collective had become. It was boring. It was repetitive. It was counterproductive, and it was draining.

I had met hundreds of new people from different backgrounds and stories to tell while they were disregarding how I felt about a situation I was rapidly outgrowing. One of my so-called friends even had the audacity to say, "This is how we are. If you can't stand the heat, then get out of the kitchen." I decided to leave the kitchen. Looking back, it was one of the best decisions of my life.

Happy Fake Birthday

The first week of the fortnight was a pretty laid back one due to the time committed to preparing for the school sports day and the absence of demand for my contribution. Despite being allowed to laze around due to my lax workload, I would have enjoyed being part of it. I was speaking to Anthony about it, and he stunned me with the revelation that he had a place on the panel and would be one of the event judges. I was offended about being overlooked as I was an actual P.E. Teacher and wasn't given anything to do. I knew the teachers had taken more of a shine to Anthony as he had an infectious enthusiasm that was evidently putting him in everyone's good books. I was a bit more neutral, partially because I was frustrated by my school's poor communication with me literally from day 1. They would make my professional life more stressful than it needed to be, for no good reason, and I would not exert myself with extra interactions with them, as it would probably result in more headaches.

The majority of my lessons were cancelled due to the dress rehearsal for the opening parade. This, of course, I would only find out when I walked to the field to prepare my class and found the whole school performing a grand march where my lesson was supposed to be.

I suffered a bit from caged animal syndrome due to my scheduling. 3 out of 5 days a week, I was up early for football coaching. I would then have breakfast and return to my room or go straight to class if I had morning lessons. I would then usually have a few hours to kill until lunch and my afternoon classes. I never wanted to leave or stray too far from home as there was not much to do nearby, and I wanted to avoid the risk of commuting and returning late. More often than not, I would go back to sleep after breakfast or my morning classes. The early mornings would usually result in a lack of sleep for me, so this was a perfect time for me to catch up on my lost hours of slumber. I remember looking out my windows most mornings to see Anthony speeding out of campus on his e-bike as a free man after finishing his 2 or 3 lessons for the day. His schedule was heavily morning based while mine was mostly afternoon classes and morning football practice. This made it that much more aggravating when my afternoon classes would be cancelled. I would think back longingly at the day I could have spent exploring the town or even another city, annoyed at the reality of being stuck in my room, killing time and waiting for a lesson that never was.

I considered not attending the Sports Day as I felt like I had been snubbed. I ended up going as most of the other foreign teachers decided to attend. I was in a mixed mood due to being on a high from playing my first game of three-way chess but annoyed at the fact that I lost both games. I still had a chance in the second one, but I decided to surrender so we could make the ceremony on time.

As expected, they knew how to put on a show. I had the pleasure of sitting on a silk-covered panel table while the school performed the actual ceremony on a cold, Wednesday afternoon. They had a seat reserved for me that they did not tell me about beforehand. It would have been so awkward if I decided not to show up. I had an embarrassing moment anyway, forgetting to stand for raising the Chinese flag and John, the football coach, had to tap me on the shoulder. I looked over at the ILP teachers who spotted my mishap. They held back laughter and shook their heads at me, feigning disgust.

The children had costumes, chants, music blaring from the speakers and an impressive formation out of the field. The ceremony ended, and the events commenced, starting with races. A few other ILP teachers and I sat with the kids on the field while we watched, resulting in us being mobbed by the smaller children for pictures as well as being pushed, pulled and tugged like oversized teddy bears. I decided to stand back up once one of the children I was posing with took a bit too much of a shine to me and was relentlessly trying to hug and kiss me.

I decided not to stick around for too long. The afternoon had already peaked, and the cold was scathing. Suddenly, I lost all envy for Anthony's role as a judge. He remained out there while I made my way back to the warmth of my room.

I saw the school football team in competitive action for the first time. We ventured out on the team bus while I waited to see if getting up at 6 am 3 times a week to train them was paying off. We played three short games alternating between the first and second-string teams, winning one and losing two. They put up a good fight considering the physical superiority of the opposition, but we had a lot of work to do.

The difference in quality between the first and second-string teams was frightening. I had noticed a trend in the lacking ability to shoot amongst children I had coached here. In terms of the gulf in class between the two teams, I told John he should give the less talented players more attention, but he did not take my advice on board. This would be more understandable if I told him this out of the blue, it could be seen as disrespectful or undermining his authority as Head Coach. However, he asked if I had any tips for him to improve his coaching. In return, I asked him the same question. He said I should smile more, which was rich coming from him in all honesty. I had rarely seen him smile, if ever. This made sense as his username for WeChat, (China's answer to WhatsApp) was "Chinese Mourinho". I added that he should try to do more one-on-one coaching, stopping players and telling them where they went wrong and how to improve their techniques. As an assistant coach, I did this a lot; however, I was not sure if he would fill the void in my absence. He was a good coach, but he had a lot of work to do if he was going to live up to his WeChat username. On second thought, Jose Mourinho also garners criticism for being unable to nurture talent that is not already at an elite level. Maybe they're more similar than I give credit for.

I guess he wanted me to smile as my role was to be the happy-go-lucky foreign mascot. I had not been asked to lead a coaching session since the first time I did in week 1. It was looking like it was going to be my last. There were even times where John could not make the session due to illness or other commitments. Instead of passing the responsibility on to me, they would cancel the entire session. As much as I was glad to return to bed, I was also annoyed that they refused to allow me to use the same qualifications that attracted them to my CV in the first place. They did not treat me as a respected football coach, and it bored me. It was easy money, but I did not travel halfway across the world to stand there and watch a coach I was better than barking orders at kids that are terrible at football. I could have done that down the road.

The ride home consisted of a team talk from the head coach that went entirely over my head due to the language barrier. A light-hearted team sing-along followed this. They taught me a song, which I think was a Chinese rendition of Frere Jacques. I repaid them by giving in to the demand of singing the chorus of Wiz Khalifa's "See You Again" bringing back memories of the summer camp at the start of this trip. They are obsessed with that song in China. It was also the first rap song to reach over a billion YouTube views. Imagine how much more they would have if YouTube were accessible here.

The American volunteer teachers were due to leave shortly before Christmas so unfortunately, they would not be around to celebrate my birthday in February. After becoming aware of this, I was given an honorary birthday which was November 10th. Because I was the only English person there, they thought it would fit for us to have a tea party. I never in my life thought I would play the role of an English gentleman in a room full of Americans, drinking tea in China. Life is full of surprises, and China's full of even more. I got a taste of a vast selection of Esmeralda's tea selection. She had an obsession with tea and collected a variety during her stay. She was also disgusted by my lack of tea knowledge as a British citizen who had somehow never heard of Earl Grey. It was not every day a group of people would give up their time and resources to celebrate a fake birthday for you, so I was most appreciative. The gesture was particularly touching for me at that moment in time, as it displayed a contrast in comparison to what I felt were shortcomings of my old friends back home.

Anthony was a late arrival, and boy did he have a story to tell. On his travels, he managed to crash his e-bike into a pedestrian (it was a small bike, it wasn't as bad as it sounds). Some drunken guy stumbled into his pathway and took a slight knock. Unfortunately for Anthony, the guy saw an opportunity to cash in and began exaggerating an injury he had sustained to his arm for compensation. He had to call Lily, his supervisor, and they managed to negotiate an agreement once they all reached a hospital.

Anthony was a gifted storyteller. Anytime he told me about a previous event in his life, the enthusiasm and animation he brought to his voice and gestures made you feel like you were right beside him as it was happening. Beforehand, he told me and some others a story about how he was racing his sports car and crashed it near a highway. He told the story so well I was still on the edge of my seat, hoping the story would end with him regaining control of his car and winning the race, although I had already known how it was going to end. Not many people can spoil the ending of a story and still keep you in suspense, but somehow he could.

As for teaching, my English lessons had gone exceptionally well. The kids are always enthusiastic, and my assistant teachers were impressed with the progress they had been making. My P.E. classes were also going very smoothly. I had put my foot down a few times, resulting in them learning where to draw the line in terms of enjoying the lesson and misbehaving. I now know how to handle each class and how to differentiate my disciplinary techniques between them. My most creative method was to take pictures of all the misbehaved kids at the end of class (the rules about photos of kids are laxer in China). As my memory was poor, I decided to keep a visual record of the worst behaved children so I could discipline them the following week. When that week came, I would pull the phone out and scroll through the photos. The guilty parties would see me do this and know what was coming, voluntarily giving themselves up to face the wall, isolated from the rest of the class while they enjoyed my session. Once they realised consequences were being carried through into the future, class behaviours began to improve. I thought it was safe to say I'm in full swing, hoping it stayed that way.

At night, I also paid a visit to KTV (Karaoke Bar). We had a local one near the Night Market, which we decided to visit after we had eaten. It was a weird mixture as Jadden, Michael and Maryn were all devout Mormons while Anthony and I were Hip-Hop heads who did not shy away from profanity. Jacqueline was Mormon, but her taste in music leaned further towards ours and Ilyanna did too. As the ILP teachers were not allowed to drink alcohol, Anthony and I shared a crate of beer, which lasted us most of the night. We had a great time, with the highlight being mine and Anthony's legendary "N**** in Paris" duet, with him taking Jay-Z's verses and me morphing into Kanye. We even got asked to perform it again, and we were very much obliged. I also joined Maryn in a duet singing "If You Wanna Be My Lover – Spice Girls" as well as other song choices. Jadden and Michael did look a little uncomfortable when certain songs were playing, but they handled it well. I had a lot of respect for them and the other Mormons. Although they cherished their beliefs, they never passed judgement on anyone who did not and in their eyes "lived a life of sin". They left early, which left Me, Anthony, Ilyanna and Jacqueline. We stayed for longer and performed more songs without having to worry about anyone else's unease. The KTV staff came in to notify us of closing time, which was unfortunate as we felt like our night was just beginning. We left in search of another KTV. Anthony was sure there was one down the road, so we walked down, growing unsure of his directions as time elapsed. We lost faith in Anthony and jumped in a cab, asking him to take us to the nearest KTV. He obliged, only to drive us no more than 10 yards down the road! He still charged us the minimal cab fee, which was 10 RMB. We practically paid 1 RMB per yard. To rub the salt in our wounds, that KTV was also closed. I experienced the absence of Changzhou's weekday nightlife for the first time, although I think it's a similar story in most non-tourist areas in China. We called it a night and headed back to campus. It was an enjoyable night.

Rainy Days, Thanksgiving and Shanghai

The drop in temperature and relentless downpour for most of this last fortnight had meant my teaching hours had suffered dearly. Due to the lack of indoor facilities in this school, rainy days equate to P.E. lessons being held in the classroom or ultimately called off. I used this time to show the children some football matches the heavily censored Chinese internet would allow me access to, which were usually old El Classico matches (Barcelona vs Real Madrid). I found it hilarious what parts of the game sparked the most significant reactions from the children. They exploded into laughter every time a slide tackle forced a player to the ground or if they slipped. They also gasped in awe of how far a goal kick would fly up the pitch. However, when there was an intricate piece of passing play or an exquisite first touch? Nothing. At least when the ball hit the back of the net, they cheered profusely. I taught them the English words for specific actions such as "header" "volley" and "tackle" as well as the names of the teams and players. I had to do something to feel like I was earning my wage as a teacher.

The rain also dampened any desire to venture out too far, so I only went out to get food and other supermarket products for everyday life during the weekdays. However, the weekend approached, and I made the wise decision to jump on a bus to the nearest mall for some sheltered excitement. My attempted shop for new footwear more suitable for the wet climate was unsuccessful due to having probably the most giant feet in the country (Size 12) and selective taste. I thought the western stores such as Nike and Adidas would bring me a better fortune, but they laughed at my request and shook their heads while trying not to double over.

Being alone Brit in a sea of Americans gave me the pleasure of celebrating my first Thanksgiving last week. They managed to provide some of our supervisors with a shopping list, which was quite fruitful. Thursday/Friday morning was spent preparing the meal and Friday was spent eating it. The lesson I was meant to teach would have caused me to be 15 minutes late, but it was cancelled. It was like destiny was smiling down on me or the school's typical fragility of scheduling.

Before the meal, we were displayed with pieces of paper bearing everyone's names, and we had to write something we are thankful for about their personality, which was a nice touch. A perfect reminder of how much we have bonded here since our arrival. I still have that paper. I need to look at it more when in times of self-doubt. They did not hold back in singing my praises. I happily returned the favour. It was a lovely feel-good tradition that almost made me forget about the genocide and pillaging of the Native Americans that was being "celebrated".

Shortly after the meal, I packed a bag, gearing myself up for my return to Shanghai. I stayed with my girl in a hostel near The Bund, which was a great location due to its metro connections and how central it was. We were meant to have a big weekend with Jacqueline, Alesha, Ilyanna and Anthony. Anthony pulled out, and they messed up their hostel booking, meaning they had to stay somewhere else. It was a great hostel in a convenient location anyway. This raised an eyebrow on my girlfriend's side as without Anthony's presence, it looked like I booked a city trip with three single girls, and she wondered how this came about. I would have been the same if the shoe was on the other foot in all honesty, but I had to reiterate that Anthony initially wanted me to go and I would have never gone if she did not come with me.

On both nights, we attended a club called Monkey, where the DJ satisfied my cravings of hearing some rap and R&B songs being blasted through deafening speakers. My access to Twitter meant I could still keep up to date with the latest releases through my laptop speakers and could sing along to the majority of the tracks played. One song that took me by surprise was Drake's song "Back-to-Back" being played. I never in my life thought I'd hear the product of a rap feud being played in the middle of Shanghai while natives and westerners alike sang along. But here we were.

Saturday was spent in a German-style place specialising in sausages and beer while on Sunday we went to Mr Pancake, or what I would call it, heaven. The weekend had a casualty in the form of my phone. After our second night was done, we got some street food at a stall and looked for a cab for nearly half an hour. We found a taxi who overcharged us, but we were so tired and fed up we did not care. I gave the driver my phone, so he could read the postcode of our location.

On leaving the taxi, I checked my pockets and felt my girlfriend's phone in my pocket, thinking it was mine and got out thinking I had everything I needed. The cabbie drove off, and I did not realise the phone in my pocket was not mine until it was too late. I was furious at myself for letting my sloppy drunkenness allow that scumbag to get the better of me. I overpaid for the cab fare and literally gave the guy my phone. I lost many of the photos I would have used to accompany this book. I slept off my disappointment and comforted myself with the fact that I had a long time ahead of me to create new photo-worthy memories. The phone itself was falling apart anyway. The screen was getting less responsive by the day.

Thankfully, I arrived in Changzhou to find Anthony had a spare phone that he let me have free of charge. Along with that, and Daniel taking me to the phone shop to get me a new SIM card, I was up and running within the day. Daniel always came through when he was needed.

December

The season to be jolly was well underway. Our group of teachers ushered it in with a mini-Christmas party, which was opening the secret Santa gifts and a pretty dramatic Christmas themed game of charades. I was pleasantly surprised by Devin as he gave me one of his chessboards as a gift. It was pretty significant considering how much we bonded over the game and the expertise he passed onto me during our time here.

The group had managed to persuade Cathy to allow us access to the school premises after hours so we could turn one of their classrooms into our makeshift Cinema. We wired up a laptop to the projector and those who were quickest to react found more comfortable chairs in a room across the hall and dragged them into the room. The rest of us sat on the regular plastic chairs or lay across the tables. The first movie we watched was the underwhelming quote-unquote comedy film "Here Comes the Boom" starring Kevin James. I was surprised to find I was amongst the minority in terms of people who didn't enjoy the film. This perplexed me until I remembered Mormon's avoid movies with profanity, so in other words, most good comedies.

After the film, we had a group discussion about what movie we should watch next. We came to a unanimous decision to watch the Star Wars series after I revealed the only thing I knew about the franchise was Darth Vader and Luke Skywalker's estranged father/son relationship.

The second week of this fortnight was a bit more eventful. After a mundane start, I jumped at an offer to play basketball when asked. Anthony and I were taken to an indoor arena by some of the Chinese teachers to play against some of their friends. They were an impressive line-up. They arrived in matching orange kits with squad numbers and everything, a proper team. On the other side of the court, we were a group of friends who turned up to shoot some hoops. It showed when we played. Although we gave them a good game, they were well drilled, and their game was polished. It also did not help that it was the first time I had touched a basketball in over two months. My shooting was way off, and my fitness was far from its usual standard. Every time we thought we were getting back in the game, they would just turn the heat up and sink a string of three-pointers to put us back in our place.

Despite the defeat, it was a gratifying workout.

Friday presented me with the news that all but one of my lessons would be cancelled due to the annual fall (autumn) performance, which marked the end of the ILP term. Instead of teaching, I spent the afternoon enjoying some well-choreographed performances from the children and teachers alike.

Later that day, I bumped into the school Vice-Principal (Principal Ma), whom I had managed to forge a good relationship with despite our language barriers by exchanging pleasantries via smiles, handshakes and pats on the back. He asked me to accompany him for a meal with a few of his friends. I had a good time. The food was tasty and plentiful. I also had to come to terms with the fact I've been holding my chopsticks wrong throughout this whole trip when one of the principal's friends gave me a demonstration of the correct grip. Better late than never, I guess. I got dropped back home by Principal Ma and met up with the ILP Group in time to catch the majority of Star Wars. I was drunk at the time, but I felt obliged to try and disguise it out of respect for their teetotal traditions. Luckily you don't need many wits about you to sit in front of a screen. Being so invested in the story saved me from falling asleep.

On Saturday the school treated us all to a trip to the Dinosaur theme park as it was the ILP group's last week in China. Luckily for us, the sun relieved us from the rainy, hazy conditions we were expecting on the day. After the day started with an average ride which trapped me and Erika (an ILP teacher) for around 10-20 minutes, it went from strength to strength. The backwards roller coaster "The Dinoconda" was my highlight. There was a puzzling sign next to some of the rides, which read the words "No Nearing", which we figured was something that got lost in translation. We had no idea what they were trying to say, which resulted in random outbursts throughout the day of us telling each other to stop nearing before we got ourselves kicked out. They also had a vomit bin, which was practical, not that I thought any rides were thrilling enough to warrant it, but I guess not as many people are as thrill-seeking as I am. I feel sorry for whoever's job it was to empty it though!

I think every job in that place was fairly terrible from what I saw. Every employee we walked past who had the duty of supervising entrances to the rides had to maintain tireless jazz hands every time a customer walked past. I tried to imagine the theme parks in the UK trying to force their staff members to follow suit. Their recruitment process would not have been very successful.

The theme park thrills were followed by another treat at the school's expense, at a hotpot restaurant. I fell asleep on the lengthy bus ride across the back row seats. It was practically empty when I dozed off; however, nearer to the destination I woke up and saw my comfort was at the expense of several people being forced to stand in a packed bus. My friends told me the locals were too scared to bother me, and they found it funny, so they left me in my slumber.

The concept of hotpot is, where you put a range of meats and vegetables into a communal pot of boiling stock and retrieve the delicious end product. It was nice, but overrated. Some people in the group had expressed that their first hotpot experience was the best meal they had had since being in China. I did not share that sentiment.

It was nice, but I'm sure I had strung together tastier meals from the options available in my local night market. Maybe I just liked the night market a bit too much. It was still a great way to have our last supper with them.

Monday marked the ILP's last day in China. After I was done teaching, I caught up with some of them and played Ping-Pong with Brennan, Christaven, Michael and Devin. Despite being the worst player there, I went on an impressive winning streak. I stayed on the table for at least 15 games and was making shots I did not know I was capable of to Brennan's annoyance. I brought forward his competitive streak, which made it even funnier when I won. The corridor's coldness prompted me to keep my hood up while playing, prompting the temporary nickname of The Sith Lord while I dominated the table. I started making lightsaber noises every-time I hit the ball to annoy Brennan even more, which was a bonus. Once I got bored of annihilating Mormons at Ping-Pong, we headed to the night-market together for one last time to get food, with us exchanging offers to visit each other in our native countries sometime in the future during our journey.

On our walk down, Christaven asked me about whether I had experienced any racism during my time in China. I admitted that I was on the receiving end of a few racially charged moments. I asked him what prompted this question. He responded by explaining his recent encounter with a drunk, Chinese person on the street. On learning that Christaven was American, the drunk shared his expertise by stating that the American economy was being ruined because it had too many Black people into the country.

'Oh, wow.' I responded.

'Yeah, I know.' Christaven added.

The fact that people had this opinion did not surprise me in the slightest. There are stupid racists all over the world. I was more surprised because I was half-expecting him to tell me a story of his own experience with racism in China. But it was not to be. I thought I was going to explore a new terrain of exploring how we had both been victims of racism in a place where we were both an ethnic minority. Instead, he was just curious about my experiences because a local had made his contempt for my people known to him. It is not that I wanted my friend to have experienced racial abuse, but in all honesty, if he had, I would have felt a little better. I would have felt a little less victimised if my experience was more common among non-Black people. However, it seemed they reserved specific treatments for people like myself and Anthony.

We returned to meet the rest of the ILP teachers. They had an all-nighter in one of the classrooms, playing games and socialising while they waited for their ride to the airport. I stayed while I could but called it an early night as I had to wake up for football training. I said my fond farewells to every member of the group before departing to my bedroom. My short-lived slumber was abruptly interrupted when a staff member opened my locked door and burst into my room in the middle of the night. It was hands-down the scariest moment of my life. I jumped out of bed, met with a dark silhouette in my doorway. I thought I was going to die. It became apparent it was a misunderstanding as he had probably been assigned to clear the remnants of items from the bedrooms the departed Americans had left vacant. I would have thought my locked door would indicate my room was not one of those on the list. As I had already sacrificed hours of sleep to see off the ILP group, I recomposed myself as quickly as possible and tried to get back to sleep.

It was a surreal feeling, waking up knowing everyone was gone. My social circle had become drastically restricted overnight. I still had Anthony and Poppy in the city, but other than that, I was relatively isolated. I started second-guessing my decision to become so cosy with the ILP group. Ah, well. It was ridiculously cold out anyway. Changzhou winters were harsh. The forecast would show degrees Celsius either on par with or higher than what I was accustomed to in London, but the air's moisture levels were considerably higher, which meant the cold had a way of cutting straight through you. It felt harsher than anything I was used to. Not to mention, my early midweek starts. I didn't want to venture out too far or have too many alcohol-fuelled nights out so I could be relatively fresh for work. I might have been able to balance both, but I did not want to risk sleeping through an alarm or having to teach a class of 40+ hyperactive children by myself, outside with a hangover. That would be torture. I was delighted with my experience up until this point, and I had made a considerable number of friends across the Atlantic.

25/12/2015

The luxury of not having to set the alarm on a weekday allowed me to rise from my slumber naturally. I wearily leaned towards the light switch and pressed it so the darkness that swallowed me could regurgitate me into illumination. With no clock in sight and the absence of natural light in this hostel room, the concept of time had temporarily escaped me. My phone laid beside me, face down. I picked it up to check the time. 11:45 am. Not ridiculously late. I placed the phone back on the bedside cabinet and turned towards my laptop, which was in sleep mode but still open as I drifted off the night before while it played The Breakfast Club. I placed it to the side so I could remove the duvet from the rest of my body without dropping it. I treated myself to a beautiful upper body stretch partnered with a satisfying yawn before standing up and beginning to ready myself for the day ahead.

I left the hostel and strolled through Suzhou's streets in search of my first meal of the day. My late rise meant I had missed any market stalls or restaurants that may have been serving food I would typically associate with breakfast. I settled for a quiet restaurant after a short walk. It looked clean, and the pictures of food shown at the side of the restaurant looked appealing. Pictures also meant my ability to point would compensate for my lack of Mandarin fluency when ordering. I opted for the Kung-Pow chicken with rice. Not my usual choice for breakfast but routine had become more of an acquaintance I would sporadically cross paths with, as opposed to an ever-present figure in recent times. I also washed it down with an uncharacteristic morning beer. Usually, I would wait until I was conscious for over an hour before indulging in alcohol, but hey, it was Christmas after all.

My thoughts drifted as I nonchalantly swigged from the bottle, awaiting my meal. I was surprisingly okay with the fact I was alone on a Christmas morning. I found the isolation rather soothing. The past few months had been awash with emotion, positive and negative alike. This journey's twists and turns left no space for neutrality. For the first time in recent memory, I felt a sense of serenity. Suspended in stillness. It was somewhat comforting.

My food arrived to my unnoticeable delight. My chopsticks went to work as my mind continued to explore this sense of stillness. I smirked to myself as I became aware of my chopstick mastery. The ease of which my food was travelling to my wanting mouth in comparison to my first meal in Beijing was a relevant representation of my adaptation to life here thus far.

I spared a thought for Anthony, who also decided to spend the day exploring another city. We had spent Christmas Eve together, making apple pie for ourselves and our fellow teachers, distributing them whilst wearing Santa Claus hats. We felt it would be an appreciated gesture, especially as they would be working on Christmas. They had spent enough time helping us integrate into their culture, so we thought it would be nice to give them a taste of ours. The evening came, and we hugged it out before we departed for our festive travels.

I was sure he was okay. He had a vast network of friends he could have stayed with if he wanted to, but I think he had a similar mindset to me; To go the complete opposite of the family intimacy we were used to and just disappear for a day. I only went halfway. I was spending the majority of the day alone but planned on meeting Tom, Mike, Sam, Fabienne and all of the other Suzhou teachers who would be over at theirs for a Christmas drink-up in the late evening.

I also thought about my girlfriend. Her semester ended in early December, which gave her a considerably longer holiday than me. They closed the facilities on her campus, meaning she would not be allowed to stay during the holidays. Her university offered her the option of a homestay programme where she could stay with a host family. Still, she declined, understandably opting to fly home for a couple of weeks before staying with me in Changzhou until the end of the Spring Holidays. For me, this resulted in a Christmas without her. However, I had planned on trying to fly home for the holidays too, but my attempts were blocked by the school Principal as I was apparently needed here. I did not feel needed up to that moment. All of my lessons had been cancelled from the date I was planning to fly home. But I digress. She would be living with me for the entirety of the Spring Holidays on her return anyway. I think adding another 2 weeks to that time may have been much for both of us. In other words, it was fine by me. As long as she came back with some decent presents for her boy.

I stepped out of the restaurant after disposing of my meal, although it did not take long for me to realise the beer I had consumed had already compromised my sobriety. My slightly weakened equilibrium was more noticeable to me as I walked along aimlessly. I did have a map of Suzhou in my pocket, but I felt like freestyling for a while. Just to see what I would come across if I left my fate in the hands of the City. I crossed a road as I approached a roundabout as I was drawn to the greenery on the road to the right of me. I saw a smartly dressed man presenting me with a welcoming smile as I crossed to his side of the road. I assumed he was another fascinated local, so I nodded in his direction before continuing to walk. He moved to intercept my path and greeted me in English. I said hi back, which he interpreted as an opportunity to offer to show me around a silk museum. I was suspicious of him. He seemed friendly but so did most con artists. Despite my concerns, I accepted his tour offer as I had a copious amount of time to spare. I asked if it was free and he reassured me and my wallet of it being so. I followed him through what looked like a small complex of warehouses and into the said museum. He walked me through the process of silk production, and I learned they produce the material from the larvae of cocoons from moths. Interesting. I was also shown the apparatus used to extract the materials and the stages it goes through before it becomes the luxurious, smooth material that graces the skin of its fortunate owner. He rounded off the tour by escorting me to the back of the premises, which coincidentally happened to be a rather large silk store.

I smirked when I had realised I was not at the receiving end of a scam but a walk-through advertisement. I was pretty impressed by the system they had going. Entice people with the intricacies of how their product was made, guide them through the life-cycle, so you feel invested and round it all off by giving you the chance to buy the end product. Bravo. I was rather flattered that my guide spotted me on the street and deemed I was a man of such refined taste with the disposable income to satisfy it.

I thanked the man for being such an insightful host, and he left me to my devices as I explored the contents of the store. I was surrounded by an abundance of flurrying textures decorated in numerous colours and designs. I took my time admiring the merchandise, appreciating the upper echelon of silks. To my disappointment, the place was mostly accommodated for women. I figured this could work to my advantage as I had yet to buy my girlfriend a Christmas present. My ideas for gifts before were rather uninspired, and I thought getting her a little silk wear would be a surprise. The clothes sizes in China were different from the UK, and I wasn't 100% sure of her measurements, so it was a bit of a risk. However, it was one I was willing to take.

While I was considering my options, my attention was swayed by a delicate yet enthusiastic voice behind me, 'Hi, can I help?'

I turned around to see a young woman in a suit, awaiting my response with a bright grin. I made a safe assumption that she worked here and replied with an honest answer. I was trying to pick something out for my girlfriend. She said she would help me pick something up. My eyes were drawn to some nightwear that excited me when I imagined it laced on her. I picked it up and analysed the size, unsure of whether it would be the right fit.

'What size is she' she asked.

'I'm not sure what size she is in these measurements. It's hard to compare without her here.' I replied.

'You can use me!' she responded excitedly while presenting herself by gesturing her fingers up and down her body.

'Alright.' I smiled back after letting out a short chuckle, finding myself in the precarious position of being welcomed to assess the shape of her body while I rubbed my chin, mentally comparing my girl's figure to the one in front of me. I had never been invited to check out a stranger's body so bluntly before. It was quite a weird experience, but I kept focused on the job at hand and kept comparing, although I could not help but appreciate her frame as it was curvier than the majority of Chinese women I had seen.

I let her know my estimates, and she plucked out the size she felt was the most accurate to my description. I gave it the once over and thought I would go with her experienced suggestion. I also picked out a red and gold robe that looked like it was destined to rest on my skin. If there were ever a time to spend on an opulent treat for myself, it would be on a lonely Christmas afternoon. I took my purchases to the till and handed over the necessary amount of red Renminbi notes and collected my bags, which also contained a free silk square I had no idea came with my selection. They were not shown on display, so it was a lovely surprise. I probably would have bought it if I saw it for sale so to get it for free was icing on an already succulent cake.

I decided not to roam the city with shopping bags all day, so I headed back to my room to drop them off. I had only strayed about 20 minutes away from my hostel, so it made sense to turn back. I manage to impress myself by overcoming my usually shoddy memory and sense of direction to make it back without a problem. No reason to stick around. I dropped my bags and headed straight back out, this time with a map of the local area in my hand. My aimless journey ended with me accumulating a variety of silks, a result I was happy with. Now I wanted to visit a few of the many gardens that Suzhou was renowned for.

I picked one at random from the map and started on my journey, walking through varying terrains. The map showed no indication of the surrounding areas aesthetics so it would surprise me to turn off a high street to walk through a township with a dirt road. I caught myself often retracing my steps to ensure I was on the right path. I was, but I was glad I double-checked.

I navigated my way back onto the main road that I was confident in finding the garden on. A short, middle-aged greying man turned towards me as I was about to walk past.

'Hello. Welcome to China!' he said to me, warming me with a smile and gracing me with a respectful bow.

'Xie Xie!' I replied (Thank you in Mandarin) mirroring his bow. He continued forward, walking past me as I began to stride forward once again.

This gesture touched me. After all the pointing, laughing and general treatment of alienation I'd been on the receiving end of since arriving, I hadn't had anyone welcome me yet. It may have seemed small to him, or anyone else reading, but it meant a lot to me. This man saw straight past the spectacle coinciding with a big black man in China and just saw me for what I was. A human being from another country, making his way through a foreign land. People had welcomed me here before, but none of them were strangers, so it would have been rather customary. This time he went out of his way to make me feel welcome, with no social obligation or for any interest in the spectacle of speaking to a foreigner.

I started to think about my general treatment since living in Changzhou. I compared my regular pedestrian journeys in Changzhou to what I was experiencing in Suzhou and realised my experiences had been far more pleasant in the latter city. I still got quite a few looks but not as many, and they were a bit more subtle. I also had not had any pictures taken of me without permission to my knowledge. I considered the fact that Suzhou was a larger city with a more renowned name and a broader foreign community. This may mean they were more used to seeing Westerners and generally had a more progressive mentality. It seemed that way. However, it was hard to compare two visits to the four months I lived in Changzhou.

I reached the garden, where I paid a small fee for entry. I managed to glean the idea that garden visits would be free, but I was mistaken. This immediately quelled my naïve idea of bouncing from garden to garden all day. I thought there were much better options to spend my money on, especially after walking into the garden. I was somewhat disappointed by what greeted me as I walked through the ticket booth.

When I read about Suzhou's gardens, I was expecting miniature botanical paradises where greenery and water would dominate my immediate and peripheral vision. Plants sweetening the scent in the air, and petals of all colours flourishing around me. Instead, I saw mostly concrete paving with trees and other green plant life making up around 1/3 of the garden. I was underwhelmed, but I had paid for entry and decided I should make the most of my purchase.

After a few minutes of roaming around unimpressed by my surroundings, I took refuge on a bench in the middle of the garden. It was a decent spot, containing a circular concrete platform bordered by trees and bushes. I spent 10 minutes writing lyrics on my phone before I was approached by a man who tried to speak to me in Mandarin. We quickly realised a conversation in either language was unsustainable, so I opened the WeChat app on my phone and showed it to him, as we could communicate via text and utilise the translator it came with. We wasted no time delving into topics. He revealed his Muslim faith and had grave concerns in regards to the sanctity of Chinese people. He spoke of the counterfeit culture that plagues Chinese commerce, from clothing to even the food. I had never thought of products of that nature being theft from the original company and lying to the consumer but technically it is, which would leave the offender in quite a deep state of sin if you believe in that sort of thing.

We also spoke about our personal lives, our jobs, family structures and other details that came together and formed a conversation. He always found a way to weave well wishes and blessings into the majority of paragraphs he wrote too, which I appreciated.

We both realised the garden would be closing soon and headed towards the exit, shaking hands and parting ways at the gate. Now I had ticked a Suzhou garden off my China bucket list and assumed most other gardens in the area would be closing at similar times, and I reverted to aimless meandering around the city.

I came across what I assumed was the city centre, as I became surrounded by high street stores. I headed towards the shopping mall, standing tall amongst a crossroads of retailers decorated with glass window walls and neon lights. I didn't plan on spending any more, but I thought I would window-shop some more to pass the time.

Roaming the city on my feet all day had resulted in the Kung-Pow chicken breakfast I had earlier relinquishing its hold of my appetite. The time had come for Christmas Dinner. I had not given this much thought. My Suzhou friends were all having theirs at a Western restaurant, which served the British-style festive feasts we were all accustomed to. I was offered a space at their table, but I responded a few days too late, resulting in my space being taken and the restaurant being fully booked. I thought back to the time I found out one of the few Christmas traditions China has was to eat KFC. I spotted the white initials on the red background of a fast-food shop with a smiling colonel decorating the sign and thought of the saying, "When in Rome, do as the Romans" before starting towards the home of Kentucky fried treats.

I had no idea what it is with me about becoming self-aware whilst eating chicken at restaurants, but my mind began drifting again. I never in my life imagined I would ever have Christmas dinner alone under any circumstances, but here I was, and surprisingly OK with it. Just as I was with my solo breakfast. It's true. I would much rather be at home right now, with turkey, stuffing and other trimmings on my plate, sitting at the dinner table with my family, head bowed, and eyes closed as my Dad's voice filled the room as he vocalised his gratitude to the highest of powers. However, I was here, and I could live with that. I was alone, but I did not feel lonely. I still managed to feel the gratitude this festive season was all about. I had a family back home that loved me dearly, supported my journey and were filled with pride at the thought of me. I had a girlfriend I was head over heels for. Someone who had introduced me to a level of love and adoration I did not even know was possible. Who had been instrumental in my development as a human being, living and growing beside me as we maximised our capacity for happiness with every passing day. I had developed a copious amount of new and exciting friendships since my arrival in Beijing in August, some of whom I would be spending my Christmas with. Sometimes sacrifices have to be made to reap the benefits of what life has to offer, and I certainly felt that one Christmas in solitude was a worthy trade-off for the life-changing experiences I had so far. Not to mention the spicy chicken burger I was devouring hit the spot. It was not the traditional festive meal I was used to, but I would be lying if I said I was not enjoying every bite. And to top things off, there were no brussels sprouts in sight to ruin the moment.

I decided not to hang around for long after eating. The sun was starting to set, and I wanted some time to lie down back in the hostel before I headed out for what was surely going to be an alcohol-fuelled Christmas evening. As I was not far away from home, I decided to walk back, only to walk 5 minutes and grow tired of map reading and second-guessing every step I was taking. I approached a tuk-tuk driver and pointed at my desired destination on the map. The driver smiled and nodded enthusiastically, gesturing for me to climb into the back before he scooted off towards my home for the night.

In all honesty, my memory of what happened after that moment was somewhat hazy. I remember getting a cab to Tom, Mike and Sam's house only to be left outside for 40 minutes in the blistering cold because nobody was answering their phones. Luckily, a local shop owner allowed me to use the phone charger behind his desk, so I could keep trying to contact them in a warmer setting. I offered the shopkeeper some money as a token of gratitude, but he refused my offer. He was content with a "xie xie" and a humble bow.

Tom eventually saved me and escorted me up to his high-riser and into his home after apologising profusely. He explained he was used to everyone knowing where his house was, so he had left the door open for all, expecting his guests to let themselves in. I also recall playing beer-pong, making the mistake of filling my cups with baijiu, a popular spirit in China that is practically like vodka but tastes worse and is more punishing to your sober state. A lot of alcohol was consumed, many laughs were had, and it brought me the togetherness and comradery usually associated with Christmas.

Once the fun was over, and it was ready to call it a night, I jumped in a taxi home and fired up my laptop once I got in my room, Facetiming my family. Seeing them all smiling at me from the other side of the screen gave me a sense of warmth that had been missing all day. Updating them on what I had been up to, hearing all their voices and talking about menial things meant so much more. I ended Facetime with my family to then round off the night talking to my girlfriend, whose voice I allowed to serenade me into a drunken slumber, rounding off my Christmas Day in China.

Happy New Year!

In the period between Christmas and the New Year, not much happened besides all my lessons being cancelled and not being told about them until I turned up at the classroom door. This was a bittersweet feeling because although my workload was non-existent, I could have spent the week genuinely relaxing during that festive period, or travelling, or going home to visit my family. I have become accustomed to the last-minute changes synonymous with Chinese culture, but I would have appreciated a heads up that time around. I had requested some time off so I could go home for a week. My parents agreed to pay for my ticket home so I was coordinating logistics with my Mum so we could surprise the rest of the family with my Christmas arrival. This dream got shot down when I got word from my Principal that this was not possible as my services would be needed here. The fact their definition of needing me was having me on campus so they could turn me away when I arrived at classes irked me, to say the least.

Luckily, I had an enjoyable Christmas, thanks to my Suzhou family. I decided not to dwell on my disappointment for too long and to head back there on New Year's Eve to usher in 2016 with some familiar faces. After a long bus ride due to the awful holiday traffic and suffering my first train delay since arriving in China, I made it, although I had to lug my bag with me, as I no longer had time to stop off at Tom and Mike's house.

The night began with a hugely satisfying meal, consisting of Thai-Indian-Chinese cuisine washed down with a beer or three. Once the late arrivals had finished their meals, we headed to a bar where we continued the festivities. I think the Suzhou locals knew the guy at the bar as we were given a booth. We enjoyed the cheap drinks the venue had to offer and played a few dice games, where I was in scintillating form.

There were no visible clocks in the place, and none of the Chinese people who populated the bar cared about the countdown. This resulted in us getting our phones out so we could countdown the last seconds of 2015 and enter the New Year with a shot of tequila.

Shortly after, the live music on stage turned into someone making dumplings on a stage and hosting a time trial competition. Not the nightlife entertainment I am accustomed to, but it was funny watching one of our group struggle to force dumplings into his gullet. To everyone's surprise, he managed to win, and we got to enjoy the results of his work as he won a free bottle!

We finished the night with a KTV marathon, which was enjoyable despite the differing tastes of music. I had to be the one to take a stand for the people whose tolerance for the '60s and '70s pop music was pushed to the limit and inject some songs on the recent side of the 21st century. I picked songs out of pure protest, knowing it would piss people off, such as Skepta's Shutdown and even John Cena's entrance song "Time is Now", which garnered appreciation from the modern music fans for how much it would annoy the old heads. I also uncharacteristically took it upon myself to perform a Kendrick Lamar song "King Kunta" simply because I wanted to sing the words "Black man taking no losses" in a room of people who turned their nose up at rap and grime music. After a while, the old cheesy music blaring out of the speakers became too much for Tom and me to bear, so we said our goodbyes and left.

On our walk, we realised the KFC we were about to pass was getting ready to open and waited the necessary 5 minutes before indulging in their breakfast options. Before you ask, no, they did not include chicken. Their options resembled what we would associate the McDonald's breakfast with, which was to my delight, as I love a McDees breakfast.

In typical New Year's fashion, we spoke about our future plans, more specifically, post-China. Tom had found love whilst out here with a Suzhou local, which had understandably blurred his vision of what the future held for him. He initially planned on going back to the UK and starting his career as a Biology teacher but was now considering a return to Suzhou for the long-term.

I had told him career-wise I was unsure of what path I wanted to forge for myself. I had never seen myself as a long-term employee and have only ever considered jobs as a way to fulfil my short-term financial needs until I figure out how to become self-sufficient. Although, I have had to disguise those thoughts in my job interviews, convincing my employers that I envision my future under their employment as a lengthy and joyous road paved with gold. I was also considering moving due to my relationship. My girlfriend was going to study in Birmingham, and I had always wanted to try living in the UK but outside of London. I was more independent than ever, and I was unsure of how to transition to moving back home. This was nowhere near a confirmed decision for me, but it was an option worth considering.

After a surprisingly comfortably snooze on the sofa and a hearty Garli Nuro "breakfast" in a restaurant across the road, I headed back to Changzhou to get back to work, or in other words, being turned away at the classroom door. Another week of cancellations followed. With me yet to teach a class in 2016 besides help with a morning football session, I had very little motivation to re-regulate my body clock.

This made for a sleepy mid-week. It was livened up on Friday though. Anthony and I were invited by one of our supervisors, Cherry, to have dinner with her husband and his colleagues. We had traditional food in abundance as well as a copious supply of alcohol. My new Software Engineer friends also gave me a Chinese name. I was christened "Wang Kang" which means healthy and prosperous king. I think I did pretty well there. Anthony and I taught them the English saying of "bottoms up" in regard to finishing your alcoholic beverage. This became the undoing of us as they enthusiastically shouted "Up! Up!" at every interval they could. We also heavily underestimated the strength of the yellow wine offered to us. Luckily, Anthony and I were able to maintain composure until we left and got dropped off home, then we both crashed. I woke up later and threw up into my bedside bin, as I was unable to make it to the toilet. We were both written off until deep in the afternoon.

When hunger finally overpowered groggy laziness, I headed downtown with Anthony to grab a bite to eat. We met up with a friend of Anthony's who he also met on his TEFL induction course.

We opted for a Thai restaurant he vouched for, but I was disappointed by the size of the portions and the absence of butter chicken curry on the menu. The waiter also preferred laughing with other customers when the language barrier became an issue instead of decoding our basic mandarin mixed with universal hand gestures, which soured the experience even more. We should have just gone to Burger King.

We ended the night in a bar I had never been to, but Anthony was a regular. He introduced me to some of the other American teachers in his network that I had yet to meet. A group of around 6 or 7 of them including another black guy! I had not been around that many people sharing my skin tone since arriving in China.

I became embroiled in a conversation with a guy about the political climates of the UK and US, who were both slipping into the grasps of Brexit and Trump campaigns respectively. Little did I know, he was actually on a date with another one of the guys in the group and he was getting jealous of all the attention he was giving me! I had no idea he was bisexual or currently on a date, so this revelation sent me into hysterics. If he did not leave in a strop, I would have made it clear that I was not a threat to his love interest, whatsoever.

Despite not being fully recovered from the previous night of drinking and initially vowing to have a sober night, we were offered a super-cocktail named "Tomorrow" by the bar owner that was too good to refuse. Pint glass filled ¾ with spirits. That drink alone was enough to tip me over the edge and back into drunkenness. We found ourselves on stage performing our classic rendition of "N**** in Paris" that set KTV alight once upon a time, to the delight of the locals. We joked that we could probably tour bars here, as Jay – Z and Kanye and the locals probably wouldn't know the difference. If the kids who saw Anthony and me daily managed to mistake us for each other, we could probably pass for either one of the Watch The Throne duo. Once we called it a night, we got a cab home. On the drive back, I had a heart-to-heart conversation with Anthony. He seemed to have had a similar situation with his old friends earlier in life and reassured me it's part of the process of growing into your own.

This was pretty reassuring for me as he had many admirable qualities and achievements to his name. To see a young black guy with a stellar educational background and experience on Wall Street beginning to take control of his destiny with nothing but hard work and the resources he had worked to build was inspiring to say the least. I picked up a lot from him from conversations we had and just by watching the way he moves. To speak to him and hear him talk about having similar experiences to me just reaffirmed I was on the right path. It was one that did not have enough space for everyone to walk on hand in hand.

Teacher Black

"Hello, Black Teacher! Hello, Teacher Black! Hello, Black! Hello, Mr Black!"

These are all ways the children I taught felt appropriate to address me. At first, I brushed it off as kids just being kids, completely naïve of their words' severity, so I just ignored it. They're just being observant right?

Then one day, I thought I would challenge that notion. A kid who was about 8 or 9 years old shouted "Hello, Teacher Black!" as he ran past me. I turned around and replied, "What did you say?" and he hesitantly responded, "Errr… I said… Hello, Teacher James".

At that moment, I realised these kids understood how rude they were being, and they just did not care. It worried me how early children were learning to negate any form of respect or positive association with blackness. Another way I rationalised them calling me these things was that a lot of these kids did not know my name, so they just called me whatever came to mind impulsively, ignorant to how inappropriate they were being. The fact this kid knew my name and still opted to call me Teacher Black blew this theory clean out of the water.

It was tiring. At times it felt like there was no escape, as I lived on campus. Not to mention that new awareness of their disregard started to scratch away at me, and I felt the need to take action, for my sanity and to make the life of any future Black teachers easier. The children also needed to know how intolerable their language was before it was too late. I took matters into my own hands and adopted a zero-tolerance attitude. When someone used an offensive term, I would call them over. When they came close enough, I would make my frustration known, scowling while punctuating every word with an extended finger saying, "Don't EVER call me that again." It usually followed with a panicked apology and no repetition. With the younger kids, I would gently pull them aside and say, "My name is not Teacher Black, it's Teacher James. Do not call me that again". That usually followed with a smile and a reply of "OK, Teacher James."

White teachers never got called "Teacher White", so this treatment was reserved for foreign teachers of a particular complexion. One of the ILP teachers, Esmeralda, was Mexican, but the kids often mistook her as black because her skin tone was darker than the other teachers. I was quite confident that the vast majority of people outside of China would be able to differentiate her from a Black person. One even asked Esmerelda, "Why are you so black?" which understandably caught her off guard.

It even happened to my girlfriend, who was of a mixed heritage of Indian and English, had been mistaken for being Black, even back in the UK before. Once she was working with kindergarten children in Nanjing as a trial for a part-time teaching role, teaching colours. When she asked a child to point at something black, the child erected a finger and directed it straight at her! Hearing about this was surprising as even I do not remember being that racially aware at 3 or 4 years old. Also, even if you are aware as a child, my girlfriend's complexion was nowhere near the shade of black that would be taught on a colour spectrum. The failure to differentiate the colour from the ethnicity was peculiar.

I had been on the receiving end of quite a few blunt statements such as "You are very black". I responded to this by mirroring their statement, saying, "You are very Chinese". This usually stumped them, unsure of how to react, which allowed me the time to return to my duty of teaching the class. I also felt like if I gave them a taste of their own medicine, they might consider what they were saying. I was pretty sure someone's "Chinese-ness" being addressed in China was a rarity, so there would not be many times they would end up on the receiving end of such statements.

There was one moment when I was walking towards the school playground, and a kid walked beside me and decided to let me know I was "too black" in a matter-of-fact way. He exclaimed my excess blackness if he was confidently answering trivia. I had tried to catch him off guard with. I thought I'd match his confidence in my response, saying 'No, I am not too Black, I am just Black.'

After a few seconds of consideration, he disputed me, 'No, I think you are too Black.' He responded.

I had to become more explanatory in my response, breaking down the fact there was nothing wrong with being Black, so there was no such thing as being "too black".

'Ooooh, okay Teacher.' he replied, satisfied with my justification before running off with a youthful, enthusiastic burst of energy. At the same time, I pondered the fact that I had to teach him that dark skin should not be seen as unfavourable.

I had spoken to Anthony about whether he had experienced similar situations, and he was also in disbelief about what was happening. The fact that both of us shared the same circumstances was no surprise to me, especially as several students could not tell us apart. I would always have kids seeing me and shouting, 'Hello, Teacher Perry!' which is Anthony's last name and how he told his students to address him. He would also get called Teacher James, even though there was roughly a 7-inch height difference between us, completely different accents and fairly minimal facial resemblance besides our skin tones.

One of the many times I was referred to as Teacher Perry, I laughed and said hi back before his friend asked me if Teacher Perry was my brother. This was a double-edged sword as I was glad he could tell the difference between Anthony and me, but I had to subtract a few points for him assuming we were related just because we were both black. I quickly told him we were not family, before the boy who first called me Teacher Perry decided to speak again and ask if I was chocolate. I laughed and responded by telling him to stop being silly before continuing my journey to class, resisting the temptation to throw him into the nearby bushes as I walked past.

These situations mostly occurred when I was in the school hallways commuting to classrooms. They rarely occurred whilst I was actually teaching. I did have the odd question such as a child asking why my palms were white and my skin was black. As outlandish as some of the questions I got had been, I felt this one was the weirdest as Chinese people, as well as most other races, have palms lighter than their actual skin tones, which was what I explained to him. I also had several random outbursts from my younger students aged around 5-6 who would randomly say 'Teacher, you're Black!' to which I would smile and reply 'Yes, I am' before continuing my job.

The most challenging episode for me was when I was teaching a P.E. session to one of my 4th-grade classes. Whilst I was leading the warm-up, I heard an outburst of laughter from behind me. I turned around and asked what the joke was.

'She said you are a black bear' one of the kids replied, still partially laughing. I stopped in my tracks and told the kids to line up. I was not going to allow myself to be treated like this by anyone. I was their teacher and a good one at that. I was not going to continue organising games and exercises while they casually made racist jokes about me. This was one of my better-behaved classes as well, so I was further taken aback.

Once they were back in an orderly line, I marched back towards their classroom.

I told them to take their seats so I could begin talking.

'I….. am Black.' I stated assertively. 'Is that funny?' I asked everyone present. The room filled with a resounding no, along with the majority of students shaking their heads.

'You…. are Chinese.' I remarked. 'Is that funny?' I asked. The room was filled with the same resounding no and shaking heads as my last question.

I followed up. 'Do I laugh at you because you're Chinese?' I asked. The class responded by repeating no, with several tones changing as they realised the direction I was heading.

'Then why are you laughing at me because I'm Black?' I asked with a rising vigour in my delivery.

The room fell silent. I scanned their faces to see if my message was getting through to them. There were the inevitable few kids with blank expressions, either out of apathy or a lack of understanding. My words seemed to resonate with most of them, with facial expressions varying from acute shock to guilt. I realised one of my students was in tears, sitting silently with a stream of tears dampening her cheeks. I concluded it was her who made the remark that triggered this whole situation. I could not have been more surprised as she was easily my star pupil. Always well behaved, helping me keep the other students in line and always brimming happiness when she saw me. I almost felt betrayed. However, her overflowing emotion was a display of guilt and remorse from someone who was not aware of the severity of her words.

On the other end of the spectrum, there was a boy who was regularly badly behaved in my classes who could not control his giggling. I decided to single him out and began to pretend to point and laugh at him because he was Chinese. The rest of the class laughed before another one of my star pupils took it upon himself to stand up and translate the point I was trying to get across into Mandarin. A resounding, "ohhhhhh" swept around the classroom before I made him sit down. Still unable to stop laughing, I decided he was a lost cause for this lesson and sent him out of the classroom.

I sat down, and the room fell into silence. I thought I would leave the children to sit in silence for the remainder of the lesson and dwell on what had just happened. I did the same. I looked across the classroom and hoped my words would have a lasting effect on them. I did not have high hopes as they would be going home and sitting in front of a TV where racist adverts would be broadcasted, such as the one I discussed in the "Being Big and Black in China" chapter. In a country where adverts of this nature are normalised, it was hard to be optimistic about their views on my ethnicity would remain positive.

My star pupil was still in tears, wiping her eyes and sniffling as she looked down to her desk. Part of me wanted to comfort her. Take both of her hands, tell her it was okay and all would be well as long as she did not do it again. However, I felt like it would have a more lasting effect if I left her alone. I thought to myself I would reassure her if she took it upon herself to apologise but would not go out of my way to wrap her in the cotton wool of reassurance. Around 15 minutes passed before the end of class theme music played from the speakers. I left without a word; relieved this was my last lesson of the day.

If I let those comments pass while they were young, they would grow up thinking it was acceptable. This would mean subjecting the future Black people they cross paths with to the same treatment. Also, the Black people they meet in the future may not be as well-tempered as me. If they go out into the real world and treat others the way I was treated, they might be met with a physical response, and they would deserve it.

I had never been in an environment where racism was so casual and overt. Before I came to China, I knew I would face a few difficulties, but I was not expecting to experience it from kids this young and nearly every day. I was exuding more time and energy than I had ever expected to defend my right to be Black and making sure those that did cross the line faced some kind of consequence. I had to accept that as well as being a teacher here; I had to also become a punching bag for racism or become a volunteer anti-racism vigilante as well. I chose the latter. I had to accept this was all part of the job.

Pre-Spring

This fortnight could be seen as the calm before the storm, which was my Spring Festival holiday. Despite the school not closing until January 20th, I was still yet to teach English or P.E. in the calendar year. The later sunrises and absence of floodlights had also led to the cancellations of the morning football classes. You would not hear me complaining about not having to stand outside in the blistering cold at 6:40 am though.

Though I did not teach, on the last day, I was invited into a class to say goodbye to my favourite class before we departed for the spring holidays. Because of a strict schedule, we had to keep it brief, but the mutual enthusiasm ensured we made the most of our time.

One highlight in those slow-moving days was my girlfriend's return from home. She flew back in and had been living with me as her campus was closed for the holidays. We finally got the opportunity to exchange our Christmas presents, which, for me, included a customised bathrobe with my initials embroidered on it made from Egyptian Cotton. This came very much in handy as my shower heater had been broken and I had to walk down the hall to a vacant room every time I wanted a hot shower. Luckily, the ILP teacher's leaving meant I was spoilt for choice in terms of alternative showers.

I was finally presented an opportunity to play football for the first time since arriving in Changzhou; with people over the age of 11, that is. I jumped at the chance after being messaged by Poppy. We had spoken about meeting up a few times, but schedule conflicts made it quite the chore. He had also asked to meet up for nights out on the weekday, and I would begrudgingly refuse due to my early rise for football coaching.

We finally met up, and it was a pleasure to be in his company. He used to live in North London, so we had a lot of common ground, and I took pleasure in updating him on London life, most notably the evolution of the Grime music scene since he left the country, which was around the times when N-Dubz was at the height of their powers.

We arrived at the ground, and it was safe to say I produced a despicable display of football. My fitness was at an all-time low, and my technical abilities had declined from my footballing inactivity. Throughout the game, I was sympathising with the likes of Wayne Rooney and Fernando Torres, understanding the pain of being a shadow of your former better self more than ever. Luckily, my teammates and opponents were almost definitely the worst group of footballers I had ever shared a pitch with, so I was still comfortably the best player there. With my girlfriend watching from the stands I was hoping I could have put on more of a show though.

In a 5-3 win, I managed to score 2 and assist 2 in my uncharacteristic stint up front, so it was difficult to motivate myself to improve my performance. When I finally spurred myself on to up my game, I fashioned myself a chance and with a moment of magic and a sharp one-two with my fellow striker, only to be tripped up by my own team-mate who tried to steal my glory as I was about to shoot. Due to the frustration of my poor performance, I was about to strike the ball with all my fury, so that made my fall more dramatic as his legs tangled with mine. I fell heavily on my wrist and sprained it, which became a significant inconvenience. I had been given four gym passes for the Shangri-La hotel down the road that expired in a month. Unfortunately, they expired before I gained mobility in my wrist. I assured Poppy that he would see more of me in the near future, whether to play more football or to just hang out.

A few days later, Cherry (one of my supervisors) invited us to another dinner with her husband and his workmates. It seemed their company had an awful lot to celebrate recently, but while I get to tag along while having free food and booze, I'd say let the good times roll. Cherry then asked if we were willing to prepare a song to sing on stage, which I bluntly declined on our behalf. It was a typical high-end Chinese meal where the wine flowed and the amateur renditions of popular songs belted through the speakers. We had to leave early as the person driving us home had a schedule to keep, which was a blessing in disguise as I was drained from my compromised body-clock and particularly grouchy. This caused disappointment for Cherry's husband and his friends who were disappointed in my reluctance to match the drinking exploits of our last get-together. My grouchiness also caused a bit of a rift with my girlfriend too, as she was seeking more affection than usual to compensate from the top-up of homesickness she got from her brief revisit home. In all honesty, I was not too sympathetic. At least she got to see her family. I felt her complaining to me about missing home was like complaining to a homeless person about being hungry while you still have crumbs around your mouth from your last meal. We reconciled pretty swiftly.

The drop in temperature had contributed to a reluctance to venture outdoors. However, the power of the force was strong enough to get me up and out of the house. We wrapped up in the unforgiving cold so we could catch the bus to one of the many malls here, heading for one called "New World" as it had an international IMAX cinema. I remember glancing at the mall on the bus when I was new to Changzhou and thinking it said, "N-Word" when it said, "N World" and being taken aback until I realised my error. We caught a 3D viewing of Star Wars – The Force Awakens. One welcome surprise was that in Chinese cinemas there are no trailers before the film, they just get straight to business. This caused us to miss some of the beginning Luckily, my girlfriend had already seen the movie in her stint back in the UK and could fill me in on what I had missed.

An unwelcome surprise was a man sitting near me, answering his phone and having a full-blown conversation during the movie. I was looking around hoping someone would show their contempt only to be disappointed, and then I cursed my inability to say "shut the f*** up" in Mandarin. Luckily he wrapped it up after a minute or so, although he had stints of unmuted conversations throughout the film. Although this would be much less likely to happen in an English cinema, I would also have to pay a lot more than 60RMB (£6) for a 3D viewing, so it kind of balanced out.

After further exploration of New World, we stumbled upon a shop named Lavia, which turned out to be a haven for Western food. I saw so many things I did not think I would see until I returned home, but naturally, what first caught my attention was their wine selection. They also had Bailey's, which excited me. It was probably amongst my favourite drinks as well as part of my Christmas tradition. Although the festive ship had sailed, I was planning on making up for the lost time. There was an impressive selection of sushi and the one thing I had missed the most, milk. That along with a selection of cereals that would not look out of place in Sainsbury's meant breakfasts were about to get a lot more exciting. The prices were inflated, so we didn't go crazy with our purchases, but we got just enough to treat ourselves up until our departure to Nanjing in a few days. My upset stomach that followed my milk binge in those days also proved my worst fear. I was, in fact, lactose intolerant.

When we arrived in Nanjing, the hostel was located by the Confucius Temple (Fuzimiao), which made for a lively atmosphere and aesthetically pleasing surroundings. In our time there we visited the Purple Mountain, which hosted the mausoleum of Sun Yat-Sen (a renowned philosopher and first leader of the Chinese Nationalist Party) as well as the breath-taking views, natural terrain and fresh air that come with being on and around a mountain. A welcome change after being cooped up in the concrete jungle of Changzhou. We also visited the Presidential Palace, the former home of Sun Yat Sen. In the palace we enjoyed some impressive architecture, historical art, and its botanical scenery.

I could not get over how accessible the terrain of this nature was. You could get a train from the inner city, surrounded by skyscrapers, upper echelon shopping malls, restaurants and bars to the mountains, clean air, greenery and lakes. If this wasn't the epitome of having the best of both worlds, I don't know what would be.

Our next stop was another familiar setting, Shanghai. We visited the Shanghai Museum during our stint, which surprisingly had displays from Taiwanese and Tibetan history. It was refreshing to see the culture of non-mainland China being celebrated despite the modern-day political tensions between the aforementioned countries. We visited the Jade Buddha temple. The smell of incense filled the air as native Buddhists burned theirs as part of their ritual. The temple store also graced us with some jade carvings that were, unfortunately, light-years beyond my budget. It was very spiritually moving. Despite the fact I am not very religious, I could appreciate the sanctity of the experience and felt the air of calmness surrounding me. I could have stayed there all evening, soaking in the Zen-like atmosphere. However, this wasn't an option. We had a holiday to pack for and a plane to catch.

Macau and Hong Kong

I was excited by the prospect of visiting a place that was said to be a fusion of Portugal and Las Vegas. The Vegas side of things greeted us as soon as our plane touched down. The skyline was ablaze with neon lights from casinos and prestigious hotels.

Unfortunately, one of the things that could have been imported from either Vegas or Portugal was the racial profiling that seems to infect the minds of some. As we lined up for customs, a Chinese man approached us and asked to check our passports. We complied and showed them to him as we thought he was going to advise us on where we should go to next or inform us we were in the wrong queue. He then returned our passports and thanked us. My girlfriend and I looked at each other with confusion, wondering why he had stopped us. Before I could dwell on it for too long, nature called, and I decided to make a quick trip to the toilet before we progressed further down the queue.

As I made my way back to the queue, my path was blocked by a short, grey-haired man who looked like he was part of the Portuguese population here. He had a stern look on his face and asked if he could check my passport. Rage filled every fibre of my being when I looked around and realised being the only black person on this flight had come with consequences. He quizzed me on my residency in China and why I had come to visit Macau as he scrutinised my passport stamps. I gave him one-word answers while scoping the environment, noticing a group of police officers and airport security watching me closely behind the customs desks. I thought I would ask him a few questions of my own.

'So why are you checking my passport again?' I asked.

'I'm just doing my job, I have to,' he replied.

'But you haven't asked anyone else at this airport for their passports, so why did you ask me?'

'I have to check passports for security,'

'I'm the only black person here, is that why?' I asked, determined to get a straight answer from him.

'Thank you, Sir.' He said, completely ignoring my question and handing me my passport. I snatched the passport out his hand, rolling my eyes before I continued to the queue.

My girlfriend asked me what the guy was saying to me, and I filled her in. She also revealed that during my toilet break the same guy had asked to check her passport too, which infuriated me even more. I seriously doubt anyone likes the idea of a person giving their significant other a hard time. It makes it even worse when you know the source of it was racism. While it was happening, I decided to maintain composure, as we were a long way from home. Having a healthy dose of melanin in our skin was enough to alert security already. If I raised my voice and channelled my inner Malcolm X to tell them exactly how I felt, I most probably would have been arrested, and the chances of an already blatantly racist police using excessive force were high. If I was in the UK or the US, and that happened, witnesses would have camera phones at the ready and people would be rallying for my just treatment once the word spread online. But I was in Macau. Nobody would have cared. I would have been locked up somewhere, battered and bruised while my girlfriend was alone. So I settled for passive-aggressive questions. We decided to delete it temporarily from our memory and revert into holiday mode. It had happened now, so there was no point letting it ruin our mood on the first night.

We hopped in a taxi, which journeyed us through some of the neon-laced complexes of Cotai we saw on the plane. I allowed the awe and excitement to regain control of my emotional pallet as I watched the multi-coloured lights illuminate the palm trees from my car window.

Eventually, we pulled up at the Sheraton where we would be staying. It was an opulent treat for ourselves after using 2-star hotels and hostels for the vast majority of our travels up to that point. We wheeled our suitcases past the Ralph Lauren store that greeted us at the entrance and proceeded to check-in. The lobby was everything you would expect from a complex of this quality.

We dropped our bags and recuperated in our room for a bit. Our fatigue from travelling persuaded us to spend our first night just exploring our complex. It was practically a mini-city filled with high-end fashion stores and a food court. It would have made an excellent location for a music video, with the star and their entourage strolling through the place holding shopping bags from designer stores. Of all the major brands and household names we saw, the one that excited both of us the most was McDonald's. Unfortunately, we saw it as they were closing but caught a glimpse of the breakfast menu they were putting in place for the morning to come.

We took a pit stop at the food court, and I ordered the chicken wings from one of the stands. I gave her one, and she realised it was undercooked after I had already devoured 2 of them. I was so hungry I failed to notice. Fortunately, she had a keen eye. It was so bad I showed the cook the colouring of the meat, and she knew exactly what the problem was. The language barrier was not a problem at all. I was fully refunded and ordered noodles from another stand. I found it pretty funny that after all the warnings I was given about China's street food options, I nearly got food poisoning from a 5-star hotel.

The following day kicked off with a breakfast buffet to give us enough strength for the sightseeing we had planned. Macau was a small place, so luckily for our legs and our wallets, a bus into the centre was enough to enable us to reach our desired destinations on foot. We saw the tourist attractions and were able to soak up the authentic feel of the place. We saw the Ruins of St Paul, Senaco Square, Mandarin's House along with many temples, snacking on their well-renowned pork buns while doing so. I also got the opportunity to buy a pair of Ray-Bans to replace the ones I had lost in Changzhou a few months back.

Enjoying the fruits of tourism without being plagued by pointing fingers, gasps, giggles and cameras in my direction was a welcome change and almost felt like a new experience. We were not bothered by anyone. There was even a moment where a woman approached me to take a picture, and I instinctively shooed her away. A few seconds later, I realised she had no interest in me and wanted me to take a photo of her family, to which I obliged. It was quite a telling moment about how defensive I had become due to the onslaught of attention I was getting in mainland China.

To my delight, there were also signs on the street that signified a ban of public spitting, stating a potential fine if you get caught in the act. The line going through a stick figure with a projectile flying from its mouth comforted me as it meant I would not have to hear anyone hawking phlegm in close proximity or watch my step to avoid salivary slime for the duration of my stay. Things I was forced to live with in Mainland China.

The evening was spent in Taipa village, where we indulged in Portuguese food. I was reintroduced to a meal I had grown fond of in South Africa, Bunny Chow. My eyes lit up as I saw this option on the menu, deeming me to browse the rest of the menu out of mere curiosity as opposed to weighing up my options. My girlfriend opted for squid-ink pasta with seafood, which looked and tasted amazing. If I was not caught up in my bunny chow nostalgia, I might have even been jealous of her order.

Our last day was spent in Coloane, a more serene part of Macau. We enjoyed views of the seaside as well as the best seafood I had ever tasted before visiting a temple dedicated to a Water God. Being two wavy individuals, we thought it was fitting we paid our respects. We finished our Macau trip by visiting pandas at a nearby park exhibition before heading back to catch a ferry to Hong Kong. On arrival, I was taken aback to how similar Hong Kong was to London. The roads were almost identical, from the high street name brands to the signage. It was also a relief that most people spoke English. I felt at home again, to the point where I had a genuine feeling I would bump into someone I knew when I was out and about. I didn't even feel the urgent need to look out the taxi window and soak in all the surroundings I usually get when in a new location because it felt so familiar. We spent our nights in Lan Kwai Fong, which was a lot like Soho, only it's legal to drink outside. That factor gave the place a festival-like atmosphere. They had a lot of bars, and to my delight, many of them showed football. I was able to finally see the evolved, league-leading Leicester City play live as they dismantled Manchester City. I also saw the poor excuse for league champions I happened to support, scrape a draw against Manchester United. The result brought me the joy of annoying a drunken idiot of a Man U fan, to the point of him storming out the pub. After his exaggerated celebrations of their first goal, he dared to stick his middle finger up at me after my brief showing of enjoyment. I decided to stand up and chant Diego Costa's name at the top of my lungs until he grabbed his bags and left red-faced. Probably my most British football fan moment in my life. The other punters were in hysterics, joking that I probably made him cry. His mate also saw the funny side of things, and we spoke about football briefly before he caught up with his spoilsport of a friend. I was in a rare predicament of talking to an Arsenal fan while his team were in a much better position than Chelsea. Something I hoped with all my heart was not something I would have to get used to.

We spent our days ferrying to nearby islands, namely Cheung Chau and Peng Chau, which greeted us with white sand beaches and clear turquoise water. Unfortunately, it was not quite hot enough to entice us into swimming, but the views were beyond my articulation and a perfect place to test my new camera. I was tipped off about the low prices for electronics in Hong Kong. It was definitely worth the wait. I climbed on the rocks by the water so I could get some better shots from my camera and ripped the new jeans that my big brother Lindsey bought and got shipped to me for Christmas, as well as losing my camera lens in between a gap between two rocks. An absolute disaster class.

Chinese New Year was a bust. We saw online that there was meant to be a festival. Once my girl was finally ready, we took a cab to the location suggested on the website, and the place was close to lifeless. There were a few bars, seedy-looking strip clubs and takeaway shops but there was no festival. We were unsure if we missed it due to being late or there was never such a thing taking place. There was no sign of anything. We got a few drinks in one of the nearby bars before heading to Lan Kwei Fong as we felt it was the safe option for having a good time. Even there, it was pretty dead. It was not as busy as it was on prior visits. We went to quite a prestige looking nightclub that was playing deafening house music. We got one overpriced drink each and headed for the hotel, deciding to cut our losses.

For me, these two locations proved to show an ideal balance of having the best of both worlds. It maintained a closeness with its native culture while adopting characteristics of its European ex-rulers. I never thought I would ever say this, but the colonisation of Macau and Hong

Kong has probably benefited them culturally. From simply comparing the people's general conduct in mainland China to those of the aforementioned countries, they were considerably better off with the European influences they lived under than the powers of the People's Republic of China dictating their cultural direction. Mao's reign would have almost certainly consumed those areas if Portugal and Britain were not occupying them. I completely understand why those from Hong Kong were mostly horrified by losing their autonomy and being absorbed by The People's Republic. For them, it would be a cultural regression and result in a loss of many of the freedoms they are used to. Such as using non-state-controlled social media without a VPN, something I cherished during my time in Hong Kong.

Halftime

I returned to Changzhou accompanied by my girlfriend after our travels to Macau and Hong Kong. I thoroughly enjoyed the getaway. It was a much needed and much-deserved break from Mainland China. The escape opened my eyes to how many normalised habits we became accustomed to while in the Jiangsu Province, such as the aforementioned public spitting and constant attention. It was the most relaxed I had been for a long time.

That relaxed mood was short-lived. I felt like something was a bit off when I first returned home. Once I had got to my room and tried to turn a light on, I learned the electricity had been turned off throughout the entire school.

This annoyed me as I had told my supervisors the days that I would be on holiday for. What made things even worse was all the staff were enjoying the spring festivities away from the school campus so I was unsure of when this would be solved.

Luckily, my phone had battery life, so I called Daniel and explained the predicament. Despite being out of the city, he managed to orchestrate things pretty well. He said someone would be on their way but broke the news that I'd be waiting for approximately 2-3 hours. I found it more and more difficult to suppress the feelings of frustration and contempt for my employers and hosts. Their levels of incompetence seemed to be limitless. After a week and a half of travelling, I just wanted to chill in my room with the lights on, and I could not even do that!

Living abroad had enough challenges just from stepping outside. There were certain days I could not go to the local supermarket and pick out some oranges without a crowd gawping at me and taking pictures. This place was meant to be my haven, where I could kick my feet up and relieve myself of the hardships that come with life as a foreigner. Yet this place had a knack for adding to my frustration at every given opportunity. My guess was they were probably used to their foreign guests being absent for the entire Spring Festival holidays. However, I did not want to spend it back home, and I did not have the money to go and travel the whole of Asia like I guess the teachers who stayed here before I did… Anthony too...

The last thing either of us wanted to do was sit around in a dark room while waiting for the angel of light to come to our rescue. We decided to take the little e-bike out for a ride around the town, which was a relaxing journey. I found a few quiet roads surrounded with green terrain that had a serene feel to it in the evening. The stress and frustration that consumed me were beginning to slowly deplete, and I was slowly becoming my old self. Making stupid jokes with my girl and breaking out into random freestyle raps, stringing together whatever popped into my head and making it rhyme.

We timed our return well, as the electric man arrived within 5 minutes of us and turned on the electricity. We finally had a functioning home again. I began unpacking my essentials to find I had forgotten my laptop charger, which was devastating. This would prove to be a thorn in my side for the next coming weeks as I would be reliant on borrowing Anthony's charger when he was around. Unfortunately, that was not as often as I would have liked. He had a weak laptop battery, so he needed it himself when he was around. I did not want to buy a knock-off charger that would break after a few weeks or order one online, as the postage system was far too unpredictable there. I waited until I returned to Nanjing so I could visit the Apple store.

The last weeks of my Spring break were pretty chilled as I did not want to exhaust my funds or myself before the new term began. One of the days that passed happened to be Valentine's Day. Neither of us cared for the spectacle, but we are also not the type of people to turn down a perfectly good excuse to treat ourselves and go out for a meal. The restaurant of choice was called Kaffa, a place I had visited twice before that specialised in Indian cuisine. Luckily, Chinese people celebrate Valentine's Day in August, so we didn't have to worry about bookings or inflated prices.

The following day was the eve of my birthday. I was in a reflective mood and suffered from my first ever case of birthday blues. I could not explain to you why I felt so down that day, but I did. From what I had previously heard, people usually have birthday blues because they realise they imagined they would be in a different position at that age.

In all honesty, I never imagined myself being in China or being a teacher, but I was happy about both of those things. It was not the usual narrative for a Black man born and raised in South-East London, and I was pretty proud of myself for breaking the mould in my own way. In hindsight, it could've been a myriad of things. Maybe I had holiday blues too. Perhaps I missed the fact that I would not be cutting a cake while my family sang to me. Maybe I missed that I would not be getting drunk with what was left of my friendship group. Sometimes it's best to just ride out your emotions instead of diagnosing it. I decided to switch off my normally over-analytical mind and do just that.

My girl suggested we go out somewhere, which was a good idea. We hopped on a bus heading downtown, which stopped at a mall called Injoy International. We had passed the place many times on the bus but never thought to explore it. When we passed there with Poppy on the way to football, he told us we should visit it when we can. He recommended a restaurant called Summers, which served a variety of western foods, drinks and cocktails. He dubbed it as the place that did the best Western food in China. We passed it on our wander so we thought we would give it a go. They also had a huge TV, which was wasting its cinematic potential by showing golf. After the manager introduced himself and we got talking, he told me they usually show all the big football matches. He said he would be showing the games for Euro 2016!! So I practically stumbled across my Mecca. If I had the authority, I would qualify their burgers as an official cure for depression. Any sadness I had felt evaporated from my spirit the moment I tasted my first bite.

February 16th was my 24th birthday aka another reason to be spoiled with quality food. After a Google search or two, we found a list of restaurants in Changzhou along with some online comments guiding us to our choice. We decided on Jagerwut, a German restaurant that was surprisingly nearby, in a complex of seemingly run-down retailers we would have never thought to explore. In this country, you have to get used to being pleasantly surprised when judging a building by its exterior, which looked like a deserted shopping complex with one or two active businesses remaining. The food was insanely good, and so was the beer. They also had a breakfast menu, if I ever need a heavy-duty hangover cure. I was sure that would come in handy.

I was invited to another football match with Poppy and his team, although to my surprise, Poppy did not turn up. Now I knew how bad the quality was and came to terms with the fact I was scarily unfit to my standards, and I felt I could just have a laugh while getting a much-needed workout under my belt. We won 6-1 with me scoring the opener and the third goal. After the game, they were pressuring me to sign for their team and play every week, jokingly unaccepting of my excuse for not frequently playing because I would be visiting/travelling with my girlfriend on most weekends. I had it in mind to help out if I was in Changzhou, without much to do.

In between restaurant visits and football, I made the most of the spring weather by going on more walks and venturing out on my e-bike a bit further. As well as finding new dining spots, I had gotten to know the area a little bit more intricately.

Then it was business as usual. My girl had returned to Nanjing after nearly two months of us being in each other's shadows. The new semester had begun, and the new American teachers had moved in. I hadn't seen much of them. When I saw them around campus, most of them avoided eye contact with me when they could or awkwardly waved at me. Considering how welcoming the first group was, I found this disappointing, and then I realised how different the dynamic was. I arrived alone with the first group, new to the place while they had already got to know Changzhou a little. They were the ones helping me settle. This time around, they had arrived while I was already a settled and established teacher here. They were finding their feet while mine were firmly placed. A decent interaction would not have gone amiss. I was past the halfway mark and caught in a weird mixture of partly missing home and feeling more settled here than ever. I was bracing myself for the latter half of my journey, determined to make the most of it.

Back into The Swing of Things

With batteries recharged and the spring festival now a semi-distant memory, the new semester had begun. It kicked off with yet another communication failure. My new schedule was sent to me 20 minutes into a lesson I was supposed to be teaching, resulting in me inevitably missing it. They shuffled my schedule, which resulted in the loss of the English lessons I fought to have. They said I could swap some with Anthony again, but he was burdened with new classes, so he wanted to get a feel for his schedule before chopping and changing with me. This was a blessing in disguise as I left my laptop charger in Hong Kong, and the postage system had left me waiting for my new one. Without my laptop, planning English lessons would be near-impossible.

I also had a payment issue. I was supposed to take a 20% pay decrease for the month I was on holiday but was paid what signified a 50% decrease. I decided not to dispute it as my copy of the contract was saved on my laptop, which was useless without the charger. I decided to bide my time and confront the issue when I was fully equipped.

Once I started teaching, I realised how naturally everything was becoming for me. The sense of familiarity with my classes meant I knew how to keep the discipline and I think with all the foreign teachers that had come and gone in this period, they were happy to have a sense of continuity with me. I had become more assured in my decision making, being accustomed to the teaching culture here. I no longer felt like the new kid on the block. I was growing into the fact that I was a well-respected teacher who had proved his worth, and it felt good. I had even noticed some of the other P.E. teachers imitating some of my coaching styles, which was flattering, to say the least.

The improved understanding between the children and me also allowed me to be more flexible with my lessons. I could enable more game-based activities without them becoming uncontrollable. This led to more enjoyable sessions for me to teach and for them to partake in, so everyone was happier.

The first Friday of this fortnight was the eve of my girlfriend's birthday. I headed up to Nanjing for the occasion, and we went out for drinks with her dorm-mates to celebrate the occasion. In typical foreigner's fashion, we indulged in a fair share of alcohol consumption without paying for a thing. It was a great night.

On Saturday, her actual birthday, we chilled in the local area recouping from the preceding night before spending the evening in Fuzimiao. We went to a critically acclaimed Burger restaurant whose name escapes me to see what the hype was about. The scenery was amazing, and the burgers were impressive, but the portions were not enough to hold me. I had to get street food on the way home to fully satisfy me.

The second weekend started with another alcohol-fuelled Friday in Nanjing with her dorm-mates and other friends. This one started at a Shao Kao (Chinese BBQ). After demolishing the array of meats and vegetables they had to offer, we headed to a nearby bar. After some shots and football talk, the group split. My half went to a club where we had hired a booth for the night. The music was the typical awful dance music we would expect in clubs here, but we were treated to more free drinks. If I was learning anything during my time in China, it was that the word "free" followed by the word "drinks" could turn any situation into a fantastic event.

Another mellow Saturday followed and then Sunday saw me in Axis, one of, if not the best, Mexican restaurant I had been to. The quality of their meals was insanely good. To this day, I've never tasted a better Quesadilla, and I have been to Mexico.

I was beginning to feel like I was hitting a good rhythm, settling back into the structure of life back from holiday. I just hoped I could hang onto this feeling as time elapsed.

Setback

The optimistic note I left my last entry on concerning the behaviour of my classes quickly soured. They proved to be volatile as ever, forcing me to tighten up my disciplinary measures to regain control. Their sense of familiarity with my methods did help an awful lot with it. Once they realised the quality of their own experience in my lessons was the biggest victim of their tomfoolery, they fell back in line. No child prefers the option of standing in a line while I await silence over the opportunity of running around outside with their classmates. I was disappointed as I genuinely thought I had turned a corner with the relationship with my classes.

Outside of the classroom, I was given a chance to get to know the new wave of American teachers at a restaurant visit arranged by the school. We all indulged at the hotpot restaurant. They were cool, but they did not seem as tightly knit as the last group, or maybe I was not as integrated with them. By this time, I had already forged strong bonds with many of the previous group. With this group, I could only remember 3 or 4 of their names! There was also a mature Canadian teacher at the school from outside of the ILP group. He looked in his 50's and was quite an eccentric character. He told stories about his prior travels and also complained to me about how the school had lied to him in his contract about the standard of his living facilities. He was told he would have a proper suite with cooking facilities and other perks our rooms did not have. I know I had a few issues with my contract, but he was lured here under severely false pretences. A few weeks later he disappeared from the school, leaving what I would call a "f*** you" note, as well as a trashed dorm room which looked like a 5-year-old, threw a tantrum in.

Once the meal was finished, I had the responsibility sprung on me to shepherd the group home from the restaurant. It made me wonder what they were planning to do if I decided not to come. I was initially a maybe, and I changed my mind on the day. Despite only taking this route once before a few months ago, I managed to lead the flock home safely. I spent the journey making conversation with my new companions while maintaining awareness of my surroundings on an unfamiliar bus route.

I got to know a few of the other teachers a little better when Anthony and I ran into Peter, Courtland and Aubree on the school field as we were about to shoot some hoops. Anthony had the bright idea of riding our e-bikes onto the basketball court so we could use our headlights to illuminate the court (it was nearing sunset). With that happening, I got the chance to accomplish my goal of riding a lap around the athletics track with my e-bike. It was partially eclipsed by how much faster Anthony's bike was than mine, but I redeemed my weak vehicle by winning our 1 on 1 game. When we were done, the trio made their way down to us from the field after their workout to say hi. During that time, Peter, who stood at a towering 6'10, talked me through how to slam dunk backwards, we had a friendly 3 vs 2 game and a fairly in-depth conversation about hip hop music. With a bike lit basketball court, ASAP Rocky blaring from a beats pill while I was in my Lebron James jersey practising my handles, I had never felt more American. Maybe Thanksgiving was an exception.

The weekends in this fortnight were more laid back than the previous two but not by choice. The first weekend, my girlfriend did not feel too well, so we had a relaxed one in Changzhou. When she returned to

Nanjing, the doctor's found she had appendicitis. Luckily, treatment for it had advanced in recent years, resulting in her only needing IV treatment as opposed to surgery. Although her treatment was done by the time I reached Nanjing the following weekend, she was under strict orders to avoid alcohol. Because of this, we decided to give the Neon Party a miss, which was disappointing seeing as the event had the expat community eagerly awaiting it. In the morning, we found out we didn't miss much, and we were indeed better off in Blue Frog treating ourselves to quite likely the best burgers in the East.

On the rest of the weekend, we spent the evening with her flatmates, whom I had got to know a bit better on my last few trips to Nanjing due to sneaking through a hole in the fence of her dormitory so I could spend nights there. She shared a room, but due to one of their dorm mates leaving after a semester, it freed up a bed for her roommate to use while I was visiting, giving us the necessary privacy. Hotels/hostels are cheap here, but nothing beats paying nothing. So if I had to crawl through a hole and change the sleeping arrangements of others, then that was exactly what I was going to do.

Grieving Abroad

One thing you can never truly prepare for, regardless of your circumstances is the passing away of someone you care about. My uncle was in and out of the hospital with a kidney problem for around six months before I left the country, but it seemed more precautionary than anything.

While I was in China, I did not get any updates on his health whatsoever, so I assumed he was fine. I made the inaccurate assumption that I would be told if any changes in his condition took place. Little did I know his health was slowly but surely deteriorating, and his demise was imminent. So, when I received a message from my Mum telling me he had passed away, saying I was unprepared was an understatement. Luckily, I was in the comfort of my home and with my girlfriend when the news was broken. I was not feeling too well, so I decided to take it easy, which became a blessing in disguise. I shed tears while my girlfriend comforted me. It was not ideal being so far from my family while this was happening, so I was grateful I had company when I received the news. I have no idea how I would have coped if I found out while exploring the city or something.

My initial thoughts were about getting home so that I could make it to the funeral. I was tied into my contract until the end of term, and a failure to complete it would have resulted in their potential refusal to reimburse what I paid for my return flights. I also thought about whether it would be worth me returning if I did fly home as there was only about a month and a half left of term-time to go. I asked Mum about potential arrangements, but she said she wanted me to stay, stating my Uncle would have wanted me to finish what I had started. I also spared her some of the details of the difficulties I have elaborated on in this book during my time here, so she was under the impression I was practically in heaven. This also spurred her to not want to intrude on my perceived bliss. At the time, the blissful perception I had been given about my experience was far from the truth. It was an incredibly difficult time for me as some of the old struggles I had spoken about were taking their toll on me. However, I refused to reveal her son was struggling while she was coming to terms with the death of her older brother. I would rather her find solace in my journey and ride the harsher waves that come with living abroad.

I suggested that we go out to a restaurant. My logic was that he would want his life celebrated and for me to live it up while I was in China instead of moping around. I also thought it would be a good distraction for me to do something else. However, after getting dressed up and leaving, I realised I was not up to the task. My girlfriend was talking a lot and joking around in an attempt to raise my spirits, but I was unresponsive. Once we had made it down the stairs of our building, I had to admit defeat and reveal that I could not go through with it. We went back into our room and sat in silence for a good hour. I was on my laptop absent-mindedly browsing through social media and other websites while I processed it all. My girlfriend just left me to it, which I was grateful for. I needed that downtime a lot more than I initially thought.

As I could not make the funeral, I thought on the day of I would do my best to pay tribute from a distance. I wore the Arsenal kit I was given from my time in South Africa on their Gap Year Programme because of his love for the Gunners. He also loved kung-fu films, so I thought I would watch one in his honour. I was not spoilt for choice as China's Internet restrictions limited my options, so I settled for Rush

Hour 2. It was the closest thing I could find that I had access to. He loved that film anyway.

Later that day, after I had finished with my teaching duties, I visited my girlfriend in Nanjing. We spent our evening at a local Indian restaurant. We had just been seated at the table and made ourselves comfortable. I felt my phone vibrate, causing me to put down the cocktail menu and check the notification. It was my brother Lindsey, who had sent me the right photos at the worst time possible. They were pictures he had taken of the funeral's order of service handouts, which had pictures of Uncle Koffee all over it. One, in particular, caught my eye, as it was a photo of him and myself in my later teenage years. Arm in arm, mid-laughter, gracing the camera with beaming smiles. I do not think an image has hit me so hard in my life. It made everything so real. This was never going to happen again. I was never going to see his smile again. Never hug him again. Never laugh, joke, or talk about football again. He was gone. And I didn't get the chance to say goodbye because I was out here.

Tears streamed down my face while I was sitting in the middle of this restaurant, looking at these pictures. My girlfriend reached across the table for me and asked if I was OK. I told her I had been sent photos of the funeral before handing her the phone so she could see for herself. Her eyes began welling up as well. I reassured her I would be fine and took a few deep breaths in an attempt to regain composure.

About a minute or two passed, and I had somehow managed to regain a decent breathing pattern and wipe the tears away, ready to order the food we came for. We went back to speaking like normal, laughing and joking, which helped me take my mind off the situation. I knew if I allowed myself to think about it, the waterworks would start again and it was not the time or the place.

I suppressed it from my train of thought and indulged in the lovely food and the company of the lovely lady in front of me. We had a good time and a few cocktails as well. The last cocktail we had was a tearful one as our glasses clinked in cheers, she decided to dedicate this toast to my uncle. As much as I appreciated the sentiment, it had undone all of my efforts to suppress the thought while in the restaurant and reopened my emotional floodgates. I held it together long enough to pay half of the bill and get myself out of the restaurant. My girlfriend, now also crying, gave me the embrace I desperately needed as we stood on the road. I asked if we could go for a walk as it would help clear my head and she agreed. We walked the streets for a while before returning to her dorm room and having a quiet night.

As much as I was saddened by the fact that I was absent for my uncle's deterioration and family's grieving, I managed to salvage some positives from the situation. However, I must admit they are from a pretty selfish perspective.

Firstly, despite wanting to be there for my family at such a difficult time, I was spared from seeing the people I cared for most in such an emotional state. As much as I would have wanted to comfort mainly my mother, grandmother and cousin who had lost their elder brother, son and father respectively, I would not have enjoyed seeing them experiencing so much pain. If anything, I would have been another teary-eyed mess amongst those who cared for him most. Being distant from the whole situation allowed me to spare myself from this experience.

Secondly, my memory of him was not marred by images of him in ill health. Lindsey had told me of the weight loss caused by his condition and how difficult it was to see him in such a frail state. For me, the last time I saw him, he was still in reasonably good health. Standing tall, with his baseball cap covering his baldhead and illuminating the room every time he smiled. He was always rather jovial and especially came to life when speaking about football. Amongst stiff competition, he managed to claim the unofficial title of the most committed and blindly loyal Arsenal fan/Wenger fanatic I knew. I still remember once at a family barbecue at my house when it was practically every man with interest in football arguing against him. It was the season when Man U had beaten Arsenal 8-2, and we were discussing Arsenal's future under Wenger.

We were all adamant that Wenger was in trouble and Arsenal would not make the top 4 that season, and he refused to budge. We were backing up our arguments of why he was wrong with seemingly valid points, and he brushed them all off. He stated he had been an Arsenal fan long before Wenger's glory days and would always be grateful for how he transformed the club. We understood that but were still confused about how he could be so confident in Wenger gaining a top 4 position. He flashed his signature grin and simply responded 'I just know.'

To his credit, Wenger did secure a top 4 position that season, and the four seasons after. I am lost as to whether it was pure instinct or dumb luck, but he was right. When the season was over, and I saw him again, he hit me with that smile again and just said 'I told you.'

That memory will always stay with me. As well my earliest memories of football when I was a child, running to him when he came through the door at my house to see a match, excitedly watching them whilst sitting on his lap, having him tickle the life out of me whenever I said Arsenal were rubbish. Those moments probably played a massive role in why I still love football today, and why I still take so much pleasure in seeing Arsenal lose. One thing I am sure of is that he enriched the existence of everyone around him and will be sorely missed.

I'm glad I wrote this. I have always felt a lingering feeling of a lack of closure from missing the funeral, but this has given a vessel to pay a full tribute. To honour his memory fittingly as opposed to just regulating my emotions while I was out in China. I finally feel like I've said a proper goodbye.

With that said, Cuthbert Prescott, rest in eternal peace. I love you.

Life Goes On

The first week of this fortnight did not provide much joy as I came down with a case of man flu. This caused me to miss two days of school (Wednesday and Friday. I tried to be a brave boy and return prematurely on Thursday, but I just made matters worse) and stayed in bed for the weekend. This was a blessing in disguise as this was the reason I was at home when my mum informed me my uncle had passed away. The second week was more interesting. Monday started with Anthony knocking on my door to let me know the whole school was going on a trip to Wuxi, and our coach was leaving in around 20 minutes. I was about to rant about the school's poor communication channels again, but he jumped to their defence. Anthony was supposed to tell me days ago, but he dropped the ball. At least he picked it up in time for me to have a shower and dart out my room wearing my unironed clothes! It eased me back into things after being shaken by sickness and the news of my uncle in the days preceding that moment.

We went to some kind of amusement park where there was a theatrical show on horseback; a Kung-fu show as well as a Dragon show, all within the first hour. Despite these displays, people in the crowd still found time to snap photos of me, including a lovely old dear who put her arm around me and posed while I was on my phone and had no idea what was happening. When I saw her and realised what was happening, I embraced her and posed for the picture. She reminded me of my grandmother a little. She has a light complexion and small eyes so it's not as farfetched as it may sound from looking at me. Anthony and I were mobbed for photos that day. Several schools were on a trip that day, so the place was swarming with children of all ages. Teenagers ran up to us and gave us high fives and others rushed to us, asking for pictures, smiles beaming and ablaze with excitement. One kid took it a little too far and tried to jump on my back for a photo! He lacked the decency to even ask, he just ran behind me and leapt. I spun around quickly and stuck my hand out to block his attempt. That stunt exhausted my generosity, reminding me that my status as a tourist attraction outranked my position as a human being with boundaries to many people here. I began refusing requests for photos, starting with his. On the whole, it was a pleasant day and a reminder of how lovely Chinese summers can be. I also got to spend more time with the ILP teachers.

After a bed-bound weekend and a much-needed unexpected Monday off, I was back to teaching, with the children behaving well except for one class, whom I brought back to their classroom after 20 minutes. Their Chinese teacher was still there, so I pointed out the main culprits and let him scold them.

With the rest of my classes, I reintroduced football sessions, which became enjoyable. The children took their time trying to dribble and pass the ball accurately after they knew toe punting the ball miles away would result in punishment. I never thought I would have to take such measures, but hey, it's China. In all honesty, I was not sure whether they were kicking the balls away out of defiance or whether they were just plain awful at the sport. I think it may have been a mixture of both! But they were taking extra care now because I introduced the disciplinary measures.

On Friday, I returned to Shanghai, as Connor, a good friend/old dorm-mate from university was there on his travels. We met up at the hostel we were both staying at and ventured around the centre of the city, soaking in the atmosphere while catching up on old times. We sailed on a ferry by the bund while the riverside was illuminated by city lights.

We had a great catch-up session. I gave him further insight into my life here while he informed me of his IT career's upward trajectory. A fantastic night filled with nostalgia and optimism. While we were on the train to our hostel, he noticed the amount of attention I was getting. 'You weren't joking when you said you got a lot of people staring were you?' he laughed.

'You think this is bad?' I replied. 'You should see how much attention I get in Changzhou! Shanghai feels like an escape for me in comparison!'

On Saturday, I introduced Connor to Mr Pancake, which he inevitably loved. We had a breakfast fit for royalty before he left to embark on the next chapter of his journey around Asia. I did some shopping in Shanghai Market before I met up with Joe and Adam, two fellow teachers I was in the Beijing summer camp with. We had a catch up over beers while talking football before we met up with some British teachers they'd befriended while living in the same town. After finishing our burgers, I went back to Joe and Adam's house to stay the night. They were kind enough to offer me their spare room, and I graciously accepted. While we travelled back to their home, Joe had asked me if I had suffered from any racism while being in China. I immediately got Deja-vu from the time Christaven asked on his last night in Changzhou. I admitted that I had been on the receiving end of some unsavoury treatment because of my race. I, just like I did with Christaven, asked what prompted the question. This time I knew what to expect, which was precisely what happened. Joe told me of his experiences when teaching and how every time a Black person appeared on the TV screen, the class would collectively burst out laughing. This surprised me a little more as Shanghai was supposed to be one of China's more progressive cities. The city has a substantial foreign influence on their culture and a large expat community. I also recalled the times where I had been openly laughed at by people here for merely existing and told Joe about it. He was in disbelief and expressed his sympathy.

Unfortunately, the downpour of rain that soaked Shanghai continued for the entire weekend, so there was not much motivation for them to give me a grand tour of their area or for me to demand one. However, the day was brightened up by being offered a chance to meet the ex-Real Madrid and Spain target-man Fernando Morientes. He was speaking at a local school as an ambassador for La-Liga, and we attended. We did not get to talk to him much as he was rushed off his feet, but we said hi, took some pictures and asked one or two questions. Being a football coach, I asked him whom his favourite manager was to play under and whom he'd base his coaching style around. He replied to Didier Deschamps, whom he worked with when he played for Monaco. I found this interesting as his most trophy-laden spell was with Real Madrid.

Where's Your Passport?

I had an extra day off due to Monday being the annual Tomb Sweeping Day, a national holiday, meaning I would have had two consecutive 4-day working weeks. I planned on using that day to travel home and rest up for the following day. In the Shanghai Train Station line, I had reached the front, only for some joker to try and push in front of me. I forcefully placed my forearm on his chest and smirked at his audacity before starting towards the ticket kiosk. Upon the woman asking for my passport, I reached into my bag for it, and my heart froze. It wasn't there. I rummaged further into the bag, pushing clothes and other items aside, and I still came up empty. I relinquished my place at the front of the line to step aside and thoroughly search my belongings for my most invaluable document.

"Whatever you do, don't lose your passport."
"Your passport is worth more than gold!"
"Without your passport, you can't do anything. You can't leave the city, book a hotel/hostel or even visit your bank!"

These were the recollections of what more seasoned Expats in China had advised me while I checked every pocket, shook down every item and turned my belongings inside out in a panic. It was gone.... You know that feeling you get... that mini-heart attack you have when you think you have lost your phone or your keys, only to find it in your pocket? This feeling seeped over me. Only there was no relief at the end. I was in the middle of Shanghai without my most crucial documentation. I couldn't get the train home without it. My phone also started malfunctioning the evening before so I could not call anyone.

I was stuck. I had no one. I had no idea what to do. I left the train station and started walking with pretty much no direction. I had no idea where to go, but I had too much happening in my head to stay in one place. I had to burn off the nervous energy before I had a panic attack. I rushed into the subway and walked past a stall with a woman selling cheap android phones—what a relief. I was not in the right mind frame to negotiate at my best, so I did the basics of marking down her initial price and then settling for whatever compromise she offered to meet me in the middle. I tried to regulate my heart rate with some deep breaths so I could dismantle my old and new phone and swap SIM cards. Unfortunately, my new phone was all in Mandarin with a user-unfriendly interface, so I had no idea if my SIM was even registering with the damn phone. I headed towards a mall I remembered walking past in an attempt to access free Wi-Fi. It saved me the last time I was lost in Shanghai so I was hoping lightning would strike twice.

I think a Pikachu had been using me for target practice because it struck again. I spotted a phone repair kiosk and rushed towards it. Rightfully assuming he couldn't speak English, I gave him a flustered greeting along with my phone. His fingers bounced off the screen a few times while I took a deep breath and rested my body weight on the desk. An excruciating 10 seconds passed before he looked up and exclaimed 'OK!' He gave me his price, which I tried to negotiate as I grew more sceptical about overspending after just buying a useless phone. He shut me down instantly by giving me my phone back, obviously well aware of the fact my phone was in critical condition, and he had all the bargaining power. 'OK!' I exclaimed, pushing the phone back in his direction and reaching for my wallet.

I took a seat on a bench within viewing distance of the kiosk, relieved to be able to rest for a bit, waiting to be summoned to collect my fixed phone. I tried to recollect my thoughts. I could not plan anything until I had spoken to a few people. I had to retrace my steps back to Joe and Adam's house to see if I had left it there. They were on day trips in other cities so I'd need to see when they got back in town so I could follow them home. I also needed to speak to my girlfriend's supervisors, who had lived in China for several years and would know what the best steps were to take. I also wanted to notify my girlfriend on the situation and get some loving words of reassurance to help ease the stress. I was going to notify Lily from the School, as I anticipated I would probably end up missing a day of work trying to sort this out. I did not think she would be of much help, but I was hoping to be pleasantly surprised.

Roughly 20 minutes passed, and I was handed a working phone. Unfortunately, it was rebooted entirely, and everything was wiped. In terms of contacts, it was okay because once I downloaded WeChat, I would have full access to everyone I needed to. I was more annoyed that I would have lost everything I had written in my Notes app, which included some journalistic entries and lyrics I was hoping to use. But I had more pressing matters at hand.

I messaged both James and Jordan about my lost passport, and they swiftly made a group chat with the three of us so we could navigate through it together. Their first piece of advice was to call the police, which I did immediately. Unfortunately, the police services were closed for the same national holiday that granted me the day off. I was almost in awe of how a country could have so few street crimes that they could stop policing for a day. This confirmed I would most definitely be in Shanghai until tomorrow at least.

I then messaged Joe and Adam to let them know my situation and ask when they would be back. Adam was due to be back earliest, which gave me an approximate 4-hour waiting period. As I couldn't afford any mishaps, I thought I'd minimise my chances of missing him by making my way to the train station we arranged to meet instantly and camping out there. I was killing time by texting my girl and soaking up all the emotional support she could give as well as filling my Notes App with more lyrics.

The next day, I woke up and called the police as instructed by James and Jordan, as last night's search for my passport once I arrived at Joe and Adam's house was unfruitful. My passport was gone. To be honest, it gave me a bit of a relief. Nothing was hanging in the balance anymore. No uncertainties. I knew it was 100% missing, and I knew I had to focus on rectifying it. Joe also came in and checked up on me. He made me feel considerably better by merely saying 'It's gonna get sorted out though, isn't it? You're not just gonna be left here stranded.'

He was right. There was a solution out there, even if I didn't know what it was yet. I could not have been the first foreigner to lose a passport here. Some sort of protocol should not be too hard to find, especially in a city like Shanghai, which is brimming with foreign influence, especially compared to many other Chinese cities. To my surprise, the police had come knocking within 5 minutes. I was so focused on starting the process I never thought about the fact I should have called them after I had showered and brushed my teeth. I was still in my boxers. I threw on some jeans and answered the door. Two average-sized uniformed officers greeted me. The English-speaking officer said hi and asked me if I was the James who made the phone call after we exchanged pleasantries. I confirmed I was the caller before I let them in and asked them to wait in the living room as I needed to quickly use the toilet. I grabbed a jumper and headed for the bathroom and freshened up the best I could within 3 minutes before re-joining the two officers in the living room.

I then took my first trip in a police car as I was escorted to their station. I gave my statement, and in return, they gave me a document stamped by the Shanghai Police Department explaining in Mandarin my lack of a passport. This would allow me to do everything within the country that I would need my passport to do until I managed to get my hands on a replacement. Well, everything except leave the country. They advised me to head to the nearest Consulate and hand over that document so I could start the process of getting a renewed passport. Once that was done, they walked me out the door. I was expecting a lift home as they had taken me from my doorstep, but they just left me outside and bid me farewell. I caught a cab home and apologised to Joe as he was waiting at his so he could let me in. I caused him to have to cancel his lunch arrangement with his friends, unfortunately. With that in mind, I gathered my belongings as quickly as I could and made myself scarce so Joe could make it back to school in time to teach. I headed back to Changzhou in decent spirits, relieved to know a solution to my missing passport was well underway. My document had me covered until the replacement arrived and that was due to come well before I was due to return to the UK. Besides a half-day of panic and a missed day of work as well as the financial hit I was expected to take, I was home free.

China Are Number 1!

Another fortnight had skipped past in the blink of an eye. I have less than two full months of teaching left. Classes are still as volatile as ever in terms of behaviour. Whenever I felt like I had settled into a rhythm with these kids, I was proven otherwise. Classes I expected to behave terribly would surprise me with perfection while my good classes would switch roles and turn into nightmares. They knew how to keep me on my toes. I guess it was kinda nice to be so far into my tenure and still waking up not knowing what to expect.

However, with the weather gradually getting hotter by the day, the thought of punishment laps becomes more gruelling. When you're teaching 40+ children by yourself, you learn to be resourceful, which for me has included using the elements to your advantage. Usually, it works for most of the kids while a few still mess around. I give them the joy of standing and facing a nearby wall for the remainder of the lesson. That way, I did not have to punish the well-behaved children any further, and we could all enjoy the lesson I had planned for them. I only used this for the older grades that should know better. When younger classes got over-excited, I made them line up in silence until they got their act together. Failure to do so resulted in them going back to class for a time, depending on their cooperation levels.

The first weekend saw me back in Nanjing, where we spent our Saturday in a shop you would probably associate the least with Asia…IKEA. My girlfriend needed a few things, so we made a day of it. It was productive, but I was left fuming after I bought an IKEA brand cider in excitement only to find it was 0.1% alcohol. As a Cider enthusiast that had not tasted a drop of it since arriving in China in August except for a couple in Hong Kong, my lofty hopes started to free-fall before crash landing into the depths of the underworld. After contemplating suing them for fraud and deciding against it, we went across the road to the first proper park I had seen since arriving in China. There was actual grass, people flying kites and even walking their dogs. We settled on the grass and eventually had an impromptu afternoon snooze.

The second week was ordinary until Thursday when the school football team had a match. The last game I saw was a close encounter with a very physical team, which we lost to after a promising start. I was hoping to see their skills tested again by their new opposition, but it was not to be. We won the game around 7-0 without the opposition having a single shot on goal. I was a bit worried by our over-reliance on the star player, who scored 6 and assisted 1, but a win was a win. Some of the kids were allowed to miss class so they could sit around the pitch and watch the game, building a lively atmosphere. Many of the children took their freedom as an opportunity to talk and play amongst themselves, but it still added to the spectacle.

On the weekend I returned to Wuxi but this time with my girl. It did not start well as every hotel or hostel you stay at in China requires a copy of your passport. As I did not want to risk losing the document excusing my lack of a passport, I took a picture on my phone to show people who would typically request it. It worked at the train station, but I was not so lucky at the hotel. This meant I had to travel back to Changzhou and back home to retrieve the original document, which was 2 hours round trip as train times were irregular. As you can imagine, I was trying to make up for lost time, practically power-walking. Funnily enough, this did not stop random people trying to snap pictures of me. I even had a middle-aged woman briskly walking to keep up with me so she could pose for a photo her friend was taking. When I realised what was happening, I pushed her away from me and picked up the pace even more. I never thought I would shove a middle-aged woman for any reason, but I had done many things for the first time during this trip.

I also had a weird experience on the train back to Wuxi. Upon stepping onto the train, a thuggish looking Chinese man decided to befriend me and offered me a beer, which I accepted. He was polite, but I sensed something in his body language that unsettled me, resulting in me refusing to sit in the window seat he offered next to him. I stayed in the aisle seat to ensure I could move with minimal hassle if he tried anything funny. He had two friends with him who smiled and shook my hand on introduction. They looked as rugged as the man who introduced me.

After some small talk, he came out with the outburst, 'So, you are black.' I was taken aback by this but brushed it off, replying with 'Yes, and you are Chinese.'

The man responded. 'Yes. China are number one.'

I realised he was trying to imply that Chinese people are superior to Black people.

'No, Chinese and Black people are number one,' I responded in an attempt to find some kind of racial compromise. He nodded acceptingly before offering me another beer. I refused and was relieved to see the train was nearing my stop. As I was about to leave, I stood at the door and turned around defiantly to say, 'Black people number one. F*** you!' and stepped off the train before I could be met with any objections although I heard them shouting 'No no no!' before the door closed. Not the most mature thing to do, and it was a statement I disagreed with myself. I'm a proud advocate for equality for all. It was, however, a sign of my patience for local ignorance. I was also stressed out from the triple commute between Changzhou and Wuxi. After all that time wasted, I returned to the hotel in Wuxi to find a new person was on the front desk and he let me walk straight through! All of that effort for nothing.

The first order of business was to check out The Red Lion, an English/Australian style pub we'd read about online. We had beers, and we ordered the most typical English meals on the menu. She had fish and chips while I had pie and mash. I thought I would have to wait till home before I had another pub lunch, but I was gleefully mistaken.

Saturday was a pretty dull day. The relentless downpour meant staying in the hotel room hoping the weather forecast of it eventually drying up would come true…. It didn't. In the evening we returned to The Red Lion for more beers and Western food, this time opting for lasagne (also my first since coming to China). After our meal, we were allured by a lakeside illuminated by bars and restaurants. We went to the Blue Marlin. Cocktails flowed, and to my delight, they were showing live Premier League football. Sunday bore Mother Nature's more generous side as the sun came out to play. We made the most of the weather by rounding off our Weekend by Taihu (Tai Lake). The perfect scenery for winding down. We eventually headed home, de-stressed and ready for the week ahead.

Good Times

Throughout this last fortnight, April showers had been in full effect, resulting in a fair share of P.E. lessons being confined to classrooms or even fully cancelled. Having exhausted the few football videos, I had managed to get hold of here, I had to resort to streaming whatever I could find on China's legal streaming sites. These ranged from recent game highlights to matches over four years old. It was usually enough to keep the children engaged. I stumbled across quite a few old Chelsea matches, which brought back fond memories of when we weren't hoping Stoke would drop points so we could clinch 9th place. The age of Lampard, Drogba, Anelka, Malouda and Ancelotti as our manager. When I played those Chelsea games to some of the 2nd-grade classes, some kids picked up the habit of waving at the screen and shouting, "Hello, teacher!" every time a Black player was on the screen. Start 'em young ay?

One of my 4th-grade classes found their enjoyment reached new heights when in-between videos, a Pampers advert screened repeatedly. A short clip of a motherly hand stroking a baby's bare bum was enough to send them into hysterics every time without fail. I could not help but laugh at their reaction. When I did manage to get outside, the lessons were going smoothly, especially with the older children. I was teaching them the art of leapfrogging and wheelbarrow races, which they loved. Their P.E. sessions were usually a bit more militarised and rigid under other teachers, so they had not experienced anything like it.

The idea of one of their peers jumping over their crouched bodies caused a bit of apprehension at first, but they soon got the hang of it. The majority of children showed quite an alarming lack of upper body strength during the wheelbarrow races. It had me wondering whether I had over-rated the strength of British kids from memory or if the kids here really had a problem. Either way, these kids would be doing a lot more wheelbarrow races.

We had Friday off due to a school sports day. I thought I would use the morning to catch up on some much-needed sleep while the festivities commenced on the field. The afternoon saw me in one of my favoured restaurants, "Summers", alongside my girlfriend, Courtland, Aubree, Peter and eventually Anthony. We exchanged stories over mouth-watering burgers, milkshakes/cocktails and stayed there a few hours after we had finished eating. It was nice to fully integrate my girl with the group. The majority of the time, I was either with her or the other teachers. Not out of intention, but it was just how our plans panned out most of the time. I enjoyed experiencing the best of both worlds.

The rest of the weekend was not as eventful thanks to the rain. I planned on spending the day by Tianning Temple, but it was not to be.

The following weekend was much more enjoyable. They also have May Day in China, so I looked forward to the extra day off as I headed for Nanjing. We spent the evening in Masala, an Indian restaurant (as you probably guessed) nearby. It was most likely the best Indian food I had tasted since being in China. Good enough for me to forgive their underwhelming Baileys/Oreo cocktail. How did they get such a perfect combination wrong? I'll never know.

Saturday was spent at Xuanwu Lake. The scenery was utterly breathtaking. We made the most of my camera and managed to drink in the best of the views via driving an electric boat along with the majority of the lake. This experience served as motivation for me to one day have a boat of my own. I had always enjoyed being in or near water but coasting on it while being behind the wheel was a new high for me. My girl DJ-ing from her iPad also made the journey more enjoyable. I came to the conclusion you have not fully experienced a song until you have heard it on a boat. The neutrality of the water does a great job in clearing your head, allowing you to fully absorb the musical experience.

After our boat ride, we strolled around the lake, enjoying the scenery before posting up on a rock by the water. My girlfriend and I managed to share a temporary romantic embrace before being bombarded by Chinese people taking photos of us, with one even having the audacity to ask us to look back at his camera! They ruined the moment, but it was pretty hilarious. We might return to Nanjing in a decade to see those photos on a random postcard or something.

I felt my morale increasing to a higher level than it had been for a long time. I felt the past month or so was pretty rough on me. The general stresses of life here were taking their toll on me. My uncle passing away was an emotional time if you hadn't guessed. The clouds were beginning to pass, and the skies were clearing literally, as well as metaphorically. I was back in a good place again.

Once hunger struck us, we headed for Jimmy's bar/restaurant where I had an insanely good pizza and tasted barbecue sauce for the first time since being here. We had some beers while looking through our impressive haul of photos.

Sunday was a chilled affair. We set off to a nearby park, planning on climbing the mountain behind it but the midday heat got the better of my girl, forcing us to have a casual stroll instead. We spent the evening at Axis (the Mexican restaurant) wolfing down chimichangas before an unsuccessful endeavour in trying to find a place to watch Manchester United play Leicester in a potentially historic encounter. They were 3 points away from winning the league and becoming the most unlikely Champions in sporting history let alone the Premier League. We returned home and watched Big Hero 6 due to the untimely death of my external hard drive. Yay.

Monday saw my journey home take longer than I had hoped because I made the rookie error of not pre-booking a train ticket. It left me with a 2-hour wait, and I even had to fork out for a first-class ticket to confirm a seat for the journey. The chairs were very cosy, the legroom plentiful, and the trip was smooth. I may have to upgrade more often.

Football in China

As a football coach working in China as well as a Sports Science graduate, I felt it was only right I touched on the topic that is the rise in popularity of football in China. The sport's profile has skyrocketed since President Xi Jinping declared his desire to turn the country into a footballing superpower. Xi expressed his desire for China to host the World Cup and eventually win it. I thought it would be interesting for me to examine the challenge he has ahead and factors he will need to consider if he is ever going to make this happen.

Elite Football

Some teams from the Chinese Super League have become amassed with spending power after being bought out by conglomerates or companies worth billions of RMB. While I was in China, I witnessed the likes of ex-Chelsea star Ramires and Shakhtar Donetsk's Alex Teixeira who gleaned the interest of Liverpool get snapped up for significant fees by Chinese giants Jiangsu Suning, who happened to be my local team. Since then, many big names have opted to follow the money trail into the Chinese Super League such as Carlos Tevez,

Oscar, and Ezequiel Lavezzi, who became the world's highest-paid player at the time of his transfer.

With the growing number of benefactors underwriting expenses for China's top football clubs, the quality of domestic league football is bound to improve rapidly. Fans will have football icons playing weekly in their leagues, raising the profile of the sport as a whole. Foreign managers and coaches have also been attracted by the hefty paycheques waiting for them in China, which will raise the tactical astutity of the general game too. The new regulations limiting the number of foreign players in a team's squad also ensure Chinese players will benefit from playing alongside the new footballing imports without their opportunities being limited, which can only mean positive things for the domestic players.

Culture/Climate

Unfortunately for China, there is a myriad of cultural practices and climatic issues that could potentially hold the nation back from footballing greatness. A significant problem in the country that is less than ideal for breeding an elite athlete of any kind is the astronomical levels of pollution. Building the cardiovascular endurance necessary to compete at the highest level of sports would be challenging when you live in a place where the air you breathe is poisoning you. There would be times where I would make the children I was teaching run punishment laps for misbehaviour, and they would return from their run coughing like they had smoked their first cigarette.

This may be part of the reason why badminton, table tennis and basketball are among China's favourite sports and the ones the nation is the most successful at. These sports can all be played inside, where pollution does not become a factor.

Another key climatic factor is the lack of open space available for anyone to play football. For instance, in the Jiangsu province, at least, I did not come across any parks or open grass spaces where children are free to kick a ball around with their friends. If you speak to any of the footballing greats, I can assure you they all fell in love with the game a substantial amount of time before professional academies deemed them worth investing in.

The love affair most likely began with them as a small child kicking a ball around in a park with their relatives or friends, eventually progressing into meeting up with school friends and local children to go to the park and play more football together. Whether at the park, a playground, the tarmac/concrete in a council estate or even in residential roads, where appearances from cars were less frequent. Clearing the road when a car drove by or reaching under parked vehicles when someone accidentally kicked the ball under one. Even for the millions of children like me, who did not end up at the footballing elite's apex, we romanticise memories like these and cherish them forever. I am speaking purely from the perspective of a born and raised Brit, but I am sure the story of football fanatics across the globe does not differ too heavily from the British. The park or estate may have been a beach, an abandoned field or some other open space I have not specified, but the premise is more or less the same.

This romance between a child and a sport is one I would see having a hard time flourishing between a Chinese native and the beautiful game. During my tenure in the country, I saw only one park that included a free open patch of grass. When there were cages dedicated to playing a sport, it would usually be for a basketball court, a sport China does excel in. The most common accommodation is residencies in high-rise buildings due to dense populations, meaning the average person will not have access to a garden. Many children all over the world have honed their skills doing kick-ups or practising tricks in their own back garden, big or small. It is a resource the majority of Brits may take for granted, and one many Chinese children would never get to use.

I also do not think I ever saw a group of children or young teenagers playing a game of football that was not a league fixture organised by a school, coaching academy or governing body. This could be due to the general lack of autonomy allowed for most children as well as the lack of accessible public areas for them to be able to play.

Speaking of autonomy, the militarised style of teaching had been a significant issue behind many children lacking creativity. In my time teaching and coaching, I found that although many children were academically phenomenal, they had very little imagination or initiative. One particular exercise springs to mind. During the Summer Camp, I trained at, Golnaz and I asked the children to create their own superhero and draw a picture of them. This resulted in the majority of the children drawing heroes that already exist, the most popular being Baymax from Big Hero 6. They also drew famous athletes and other film characters. In football, you can only coach so much, and you cannot coach the flair necessary to match the heights of Ronaldo, Neymar or Messi. With most Chinese youth being so reliant on authority and following instructions, I doubt it would translate well on the football pitch where there are many split-second decisions a player needs to make throughout a match.

During one of my coaching sessions, the head coach, John, taught one of the children the stepover. (I'm guessing anyone who doesn't know what a stepover is has skipped this chapter) When he practised the skill, he was going through the motions while running straight into me, at the expense of my toes once his studs crunched into them. With most kids, their initiative would have kicked in, and they would have done fewer stepovers and tapped the ball around me once they realised how close they were getting to my feet. I saw this moment as the perfect manifestation of my concerns for their over-reliance on instructions.

For anything to change in this department, it would take an almighty cultural shift across the country regarding their education, workplace hierarchy and even their governmental structure. The nation as a whole is reliant on an authoritative approach whenever a hierarchy is involved. As much as Xi Jinping loves football, I doubt he would be willing to loosen up the iron-fisted grip his government has on China's people.

Conclusion

For China to become even remotely competitive on a global scale, they have a lot of work to do from the ground up. They have astronomical financial backing at the elite level and a government willing to prioritise resources to facilitate the growth of the sport. As positive as this is, it will not be enough alone. Football is different from many of the sports that Chinese athletes have previously conquered.

For a country's national team to be successful, it must be culturally intertwined with its people. The sport has to be accessible to maximise the probability of potential superstars discovering their passion for the game and their ability to pursue their dream of playing their way into the apex of it. With the lack of open spaces in China for children to hone their skills, there would be a struggle to meet the accessibility to the sport needed for Chinese footballers to thrive on a global scale.

Although China has a powerful national identity, players need to be able to express themselves individually and master their sense of autonomy when they are competing. An outside influence will facilitate that majorly.

Humanitarian Hitler?

As expected, the workload had slightly decreased as we moved towards the academic year's final month. It was insane how fast this year had gone. I felt like the most challenging parts of the journey were behind me. Any disciplinary issues I may have had with classes did not matter. The classes' mentality was more laid back and the fact I would be gone from the school in less than two months with no desire to return meant I loosened my usually stringent rules.

Classes had been rehearsing for their end of year performances and ceremonies, meaning a few of my lessons had been cancelled. As always, I did not find out about these cancellations until I walked into an empty classroom. Either that or the kids saw me approaching through the window and signalled that my services were not required. Although I was used to it, I really would appreciate the extra hours of uninterrupted sleep or the freedom to plan for the day.

The first weekend began with a meal at Kaffa, a nearby Indian restaurant with Anthony. We were promised a free meal there as the last time we ate a meal there we both fell ill for a few days. We gave them a chance to redeem themselves, as their food was usually top quality. It became the perfect way to start Anthony's birthday celebrations. At the table, I met Jong-Ho (I think that's how you spell it) a friend of Anthony's, a Kung Fu enthusiast and a lovely guy. He said he would be more than happy to do Kung Fu with us. Unfortunately, he had to leave before the food arrived and left us to eat while adding celebratory beers to the occasion. We ended up over-ordering and invited Poppy along to help us finish our meal.

Anthony was sceptical about his birthday plans, so after the meal, I headed up to Nanjing to see my girl. I harassed Anthony for details on how he planned to celebrate his birthday, as I wanted to be there with him. He said he did not have the slightest clue and advised me to go to Nanjing. He did not want me to potentially stick around for nothing, so I left him to it. He went on to hit a few bars in town and had a boozy night. I was upset to hear I missed out. Ah, well. As long as the birthday boy was happy, that's all that matters.

The highlight of the weekend was trying my hand at badminton for the first time. My girl got back into the swing of it with her friend and offered to show me the ropes. They had courts on their campus, so we put them to use. I caught on pretty quickly being the finely tuned athlete and generally incredible human being that I am. She was surprised with how hard I made her work to keep rallies going. Eventually, she upped the levels and killed me with drop shots at every opportunity to show me who was boss. She said we were evenly matched, though. I developed quite a mean drop shot myself. My Dad's pretty handy on the badminton court too. Maybe it was in the blood.

We rounded off the night with dinner at Jimmy's bar. Man U - Norwich were on the telly, which was pleasing yet annoying at the same time, as I found the perfect weekend bar to watch football the week before the season ended. Maybe the gods were trying to protect my fragile heart from witnessing Chelsea's downfall game by game. I was optimistic I would catch some of the European Championships there though.

I decided to meet up with Jong-Ho after I had finished my teaching duties for the day and tried my hand at some Kung Fu, which had been a dream for me since arriving in China. He was studying in a local university, which was about a 10-minute e-bike ride away, so I scooted there, whizzing past security uninterrupted once I reached their gates.

I met him on their sports ground/arena that was brimming with life. Dance classes were practising their moves as well as gymnasts working through their stretches. Another Kung-Fu class was also there, practising actual martial arts as well as ceremonial pattern sequences, involving some impressive manoeuvres with nunchucks, sticks and spears.

I was raring to go. I quickly learned how technical every movement had to be and how so much stemmed from having the right stance. The power of each strike comes from the use of the whole body. I was also intrigued by how he demonstrated using physical inferiority to your advantage. He would encourage me to get him in holds before effortlessly reversing them, leaving me vulnerable to strike attacks, submissions, or both. He explained that it always helped to be stronger than your opponent, but despite being used to having an advantage in size, I also need to know how to manoeuvre when it was not the case.

Moreover, he showed me a meditation technique to "realign my chi". I must say I felt centred and relaxed afterwards and have every intention of maintaining the habit. He is originally from Anhui, but we were both staying in Changzhou until July, and he said that would be enough time to give me a healthy repertoire of moves. I looked forward to learning more.

The following day, after recently trying my hand at a new sport and martial art, I returned to my first love. Football. Poppy's friends had a kickabout at a local 5 a side pitch, so I went to meet him with Anthony and Jake, an ILP Teacher from the school. We were on the same team plus a Chinese player, which meant hard work for Poppy and me, as Anthony and Jake had never played football before. They worked hard and started to get the hang of the basics as I tried to talk them through the game. Anthony was fast and agile while Jake was fearless in his tackles and not afraid to impose himself. I also felt that with two rookies in our team, I had the motivation to up my game to compensate for the gulf in quality.

We became quite a formidable force. They worked hard off the ball and made some tackles, kept it simple and even bagged a few goals. I enjoyed it much more than my other times playing football out here, as I was among good friends. It also helped that Jake and Anthony knew they were not good players and determined to improve their game as opposed to awful players who thought they were the next Messi, carrying around unwarranted egos. The cultural differences also showed with the opposition as they complained after every tackle I made despite me winning the ball. Poppy, who had lived in the UK before, told me the styles of play were utterly different in China.

'I promise you, they've never been tackled like that in their lives' he laughed.

I could see that being true, as many British players I've faced could also say the same thing. I joked and said if Xi Jinping ever wants his football dreams to come true, they need to learn how the rest of the world plays, the hard way.

At the weekend I found myself back in Nanjing where the highlight was visiting the bluntly named "Memorial Hall of The Victims In Nanjing Massacre by Japanese Invaders". I was taken aback by the name's directness and how bare the atrocities were laid for all to see. It was a clear indicator of how the writers of history have the power to influence perception. As we were in China, and they were the unfortunate victims of this massacre, they held nothing back in their attempts to expose the evil the Japanese put them on the receiving end of. The contrast was stark when you compare narratives on slavery or The British Empire in the UK. There was usually a lighter tone, or nuanced language used when telling that tale, as the British, Europeans and Americans are reluctant to paint themselves in a villainous light despite their actions earning such imagery. I am sure if slaves or the victims of the British Empire had the freedom and resources to curate a museum dedicated to their own suffering, it would look very similar to what I was witnessing in Nanjing.

There was some very emotionally provocative artwork, imagery and descriptions of the atrocities that occurred. Moreover, we found some fascinating occurrences such as Adolf Hitler's humanitarian aid of the Chinese victims. As someone born and raised in Britain, the last word I would associate with Adolf Hitler was humanitarian. However, he played an integral part in giving aid, manpower and resources to China to facilitate their recovery from the massacre. Another example of how different perception can be depending on where you are brought up.

However, the day did have its annoyances. We were being followed by groups of Chinese teens who were trying to take pictures and generally observe us. It got to the point where I had to shoo them off, either walking up to them and pointing away or lowering their phones myself. In a crowd of 20/30, you had to concede defeat, but I took action when I could. With some people, I pointed my camera towards them, and they genuinely thought I wanted to shoot them, proceeding to try and befriend me, which was met with being ignored. They got the message eventually. We got some memorable photos too, including one of the statues representing peace. After such events, it was inspiring to see the memorial's underlying message was one seeking harmony. If only the Chinese media shared this sentiment. Many of their most famous action shows/movies revolve around a war hero killing Japanese soldiers, as viewers live vicariously through them. A very lucrative role in the Chinese TV/Film industry is a Japanese extra that gets killed off by the main character due to the extensive demand.

Smile for The Camera

A couple of factors heavily contributed to my change of mentality towards the native happy snappers. The first one was simply because it was annoying. The novelty was always going to wear off sooner or later and once it did the levels of irritation multiplied significantly. When you are new to a country, the euphoria triggered from the excitement and myriad of new experiences happening at once can easily cause one to glaze over anything you may potentially perceive as annoying. But once that thrill is gone, the euphoria fades. You are simply a foreign worker, stressed from a long day of work, doing your weekly shop and some random person with a goofy smile points a camera-phone in your direction. At the same time, you try to pick out some oranges, and the experience is digested a little differently. In their eyes, I felt like a walking freak show. People were reacting to me as if a walrus were making their way around the supermarket. I am sure if I walked around London wearing pink hot pants and green cowboy boots while wearing a "Make America Great Again" hat, people would still be subtler than what was happening here.

I had received paparazzi-like attention during my first tourist outings in China, exploring Beijing's with the rest of the fresh batch of teachers. However, my perspective had shifted majorly. At first, I found it quite funny. I enjoyed the attention as I found their reactions to me entertaining as opposed to flattering, but I enjoyed it nonetheless. When I had time, I posed for any photo that was asked of me, holding babies, putting my arm around old ladies and throwing up their renowned peace signs. As time progressed my accommodating demeanour slowly deteriorated.

Another triggering factor was my ever-sceptical thought process beginning to dissect why they had any desire to take pictures of me in the first place. This was triggered early on when I was walking around with some of the ILP teachers. One of the teachers, Esmeralda, was reasonably fluent in Mandarin. She would probably deny fluency if asked but compared to the rest of us she may as well have been born and raised in the heart of Beijing. As she was Mexican, many Chinese people would make passing comments in her proximity and think she was oblivious when she understood perfectly. One pattern that sparked a curiosity within me was the exchanges parents and children would make when the parent would ask one of us for a picture. While we thought children were reluctant to take photos with us because they were shy, they were saying to their parents 'I don't want to take a picture, you told me that foreign people are devils. I don't want to go near them.' Or statements along those lines.

This was weird to me. In all honesty, the child in that situation would be right. If I had been told all my life that a particular type of person were devils, the last thing I would want was for one of them to put my arm around me for a photo. This revelation also thoroughly washed away the glossy preconception of "celebrity treatment" I may have had beforehand. With that said, I am not sure how typical this mentality is so I would have to be careful with the number of people I stroke with my tarred brush.

Nonetheless, it was a noteworthy observation. The comments weren't always nasty. Once my girl's Mandarin lessons were in full swing, she also managed to pick up on a few compliments being uttered in our direction, mostly variations of the pair of us being called tall and beautiful/handsome.

Towards the end of my tenure, it became more and more tiresome trying to differentiate who was genuinely interested in meeting and greeting a foreigner or who just wanted a picture with a "devil". I would still stop for photos when asked nicely enough. However, I was a lot more hostile to people taking pictures without my permission. I would shoot them a menacing look or even go as far as taking phones from hands so I could delete their photos myself. The first time I had done as such, I had taken a look at their picture just to see what the fuss was about. Seeing my nonchalant self in mid-stride being viewed as a Kodak moment was a weird feeling. There was absolutely nothing special about this photo. I was just walking. The thought of her posting a picture of me walking on her social network or showing it to her friends was just unfathomable to me.

After further thought, I considered that modern Chinese culture does somewhat revolve around capturing near enough every part of your day behind a lens. If any country has embraced social media to its full extent, it's China. They do not miss the likes of Twitter or Instagram in terms of keeping up to date with each other as they have their alternatives, such as WeChat and Weibo, to name a couple.

For those who had found it necessary to take a picture of me, I would probably be one of 10 images that day. On my way to work selfie, noodles for lunch, walked past a big black guy, afternoon conference, etc. Either way, the cameras pointing my way for no good reason wasn't something I could get used to. Many were flattered by the attention, but I found it dehumanising and disrespectful, especially those who pulled their cameras out and took pictures without giving me a choice in the matter.

Shanghai Goodbyes and Euro 16

The end was fast approaching. Honestly, it already felt like my work here was done, as nearing exams had resulted in most of my classes' cancellation. I could count the lessons I had taught in the last fortnight on the one hand, and in all honesty, I could only see the number decreasing from there.

The first weekend I headed for Suzhou to meet up with Tom. Saturday was scheduled as the Suzhou crew's last night out together in Shanghai, so I thought I would crash at Tom's the night before so we could make our way up together. We had a lad's night in, playing Star Wars Battlefront and watching Creed while eating pizza and drinking beer.

Saturday was fun. The tone was set once Emily and Peter pulled out two six-packs of beer just as we sat on the train, making us feel stereotypically British. My mood was soured when I learned of the passing of one of my lifelong heroes, Muhammad Ali. I was cut deep by this revelation. In all honesty, if I were back in Changzhou, I would have stayed at home, watched old videos of his boxing matches and interviews while mourning the loss of a great man. This was not a reasonable option for me as I was already on a train to Shanghai.

We carried on drinking and playing card games once we arrived at the hostel and made the most of their happy hour in the hostel bar, racking up orders of cocktails and beers.

The intensity stepped up at sunset, preparing us for a night out on the town, which involved balloon animals and dancing on the bar with cocktails in our hands. The night took a nosedive once the DJ ruined everything with his music selection. I sat outside by the tables for the next hour, engaging in conversations with the others while we all hoped the music would pick up again.

One of our group had managed to befriend a Chinese woman whose name I was too drunk to keep track of. She boasted excellent English and hung out with our group. She told us about the business connections she had in Shanghai and said that she would probably be able to hook us up with jobs if we wanted, as English speakers were in high demand. Luckily for me, the prospect did not excite me, as she immediately apologised to me, before explaining that her connections would not be interested in hiring anyone Black. I put her at ease, telling her not to apologise as it was not her fault that her colleagues were racist. I was rather grateful she said it so bluntly, as one of the people in our pre-drinking group had earlier challenged me on why I talk about racism so much. She helped prove my point. The rest of the night was forgettable. The music remained terrible, and we went back to our hostel. Overall, it was fun.

The following week accounted for 0% of my teaching time. My lessons were all cancelled Monday-Wednesday, and the rest of the week was a national holiday known as the Dragon Boat Festival.

Friday, I headed for Nanjing. My girlfriend was back from her trip to Chengdu, so we had a day out/catch up session. We went to the Purple Mountain to see the Xiaoling Mausoleum of the Ming Dynasty. The scenery was a blend of incredible sculptings and flourishing greenery that kept my camera busy. Afterwards, we headed for our second home, Jimmy's bar. We filled up on pizzas and beers before going back to Changzhou.

Saturday night we went to a Chinese bar after Poppy messaged me his plans to get people together so we could watch the Euro 2016 fixtures. We were given the immediate celebrity treatment of free drinks, unauthorised photos in addition to one of the punters comedically pulling up a chair in front of us so he could watch us while the football was playing right behind him!

I was glad the chance to have a proper catch up with Anthony had presented itself. It was the first time I had seen him in nearly two weeks. He was always off-campus socialising or following up on entrepreneurial endeavours, so it was normal to not see him every day. However, I was a little concerned as he had been uncharacteristically quiet. I found out he had to go back to the States for a bit due to an emergency at home. He had returned on the day only to go straight into working on his business ventures. He looked exhausted, and I understood why.

The midnight fixture of Wales vs Slovakia was finished so we got a late-night snack from McDonald's before switching our location to Summer's to watch England vs Russia. We had a few more free beers and met three or four other English immigrants. It proved to be too much to ask of Anthony as he went home early. My girlfriend was also falling asleep on my shoulder by half time. After watching England succumb to a late equaliser, it was home time. Because I had days off for the Dragon Boat Festival, the school was running on Sunday, meaning I was dreading the thought of teaching classes with under 2 hours sleep.

In the cab home, I spoke to Poppy about the poor communication from the teachers here. He said it's because people here expect to be brown-nosed before they make even the most minimal effort with working towards your convenience. He commended me for not stooping to that level. Sucking up to people has never been in my nature, and it never will. I would rather cut my nose to spite my face than brown-nose my way into anyone's good books. I was glad he helped me make sense of the whole fiasco, but I regret nothing. The trend of cancelled lessons continued, so I went back to bed and slept till the mid-afternoon, waking up with another day to kill.

Warming Down

As I expected, my working hours were reduced to zero for my final two weeks as an English teacher in China. I did not bother to turn up as I felt it was a waste of time venturing to the classrooms only to get waved away. I also thought if there was the off chance of my class being scheduled for me to teach, the volume of cancelled lessons would quickly validate my absence.

During the week I met Poppy outside the local Injoy shopping centre after he finished work so we could watch England vs Wales at Summer's. He was nice enough to give me a lift on the back of his e-bike. Well, after realising the length of my legs would mean I would be more comfortable in the front, he let me drive while directing from the rear. It was an enjoyable experience as his e-moped was much bigger, faster and more powerful than my little scooter, although not having a helmet made me slightly uneasy (Sorry, Mum). The wind blowing felt terrific as it was a relatively humid summer evening as we raced down the bustling roads.

We made it in one piece after 30-minute ride downtown. The atmosphere in Summer's was electric as quite a few English people turned up and livened the place up. Some were a little too lively. I have to wonder why the loudest people amongst a crowd of people watching football are usually the ones who know the least about the beautiful game. Shouting awful coaching advice at the screen while giving a running commentary that nobody asked for. One guy also made an ignorant comment about the Wales player Hal Robson-Kanu, mentioning his name not being "very Welsh". Considering that Robson is a Welsh name I could only assume he took issue with the Nigerian side of his name "Kanu". It was pretty surprising that a white Englishman who was living in China could take issue with a person with half Nigerian heritage representing a British country. Mentalities like that are far too common amongst English people and a big reason why I'm not very patriotic. My apathy for England became my undoing. In the 90th minute, I bet Poppy that England would not score again, only for Poppy's blind faith to pay off as Daniel Sturridge scored the winning goal about 30 seconds later. I laughed in disbelief as the whole place cheered hysterically, ridiculed me, and for a good reason. At least the bet was only for 1 RMB (10p).

My Kung Fu buddy Jong-Ho messaged me saying he was back in town and wanted to treat Anthony and me to some Indian food at Kaffa, the Indian restaurant we first met on Anthony's birthday; how sentimental. It was a good meal despite the dip in service quality from prior visits. I ordered one mango lassi and was given 3. It would've made sense if there was one each, but there were 5 of us, so there was no reason for her to think anyone ordered 3. They also gave us a lamb roganjosh we didn't order.

When we asked him to take it back, he said it was too late because we had already touched it. Anthony and I reiterated that it was still untampered with and he stared blankly, before walking away and leaving it on the table. Being the Kung-Fu enthusiast he is, Jong-Ho still managed to give Anthony and I a quick tutorial by the table on how to harness our inner power through meditation. Nourishing us with food and wisdom, I picked a great Chinese best friend.

Farewell Changzhou, Teacher Black No More!

The following week was my last in Changzhou. It felt surreal that I was gearing up to leave what had been my home for the previous ten months. I was going to be ending a job my life revolved around for the last ten months. I spent it visiting some of my favourite restaurants for the last time. I also had a final visit to the night market that fed me for the duration of my stay while the school provided meals did not quite cut it. I brought my camera out to mark the occasion, but the air was so humid my lens fogged up within seconds! I had never seen anything like it. It was a shame I did not think to capture these moments sooner. I would now have to rely purely on memory.

I had my last Kung Fu lesson, where I practised using my "inner power" along with some techniques I had previously used. Jong-Ho bought me a gift in the form of a necklace with a pendant of a warrior dangling from it. He said it was a special gift from master to student representing courage and loyalty. I was happy with the depiction, but I also felt guilty. I did not get him anything to remember me by. I was touched by the sentiment of the gift and very happy that as an accessory, I could pull it off too. I was silly enough to think he wanted to just meet up and chill, but he made me do a full session. I was dressed casually and had a belly full of Burger King, as I had eaten two meals there an hour or so ago. I fought through the bloat and gave it everything I could, successfully avoiding any visual sluggishness.

Unfortunately, the majority of the American volunteer teachers had already set off on their travels. They would not be back until after I had left, so I did not get to say a proper goodbye to them. It also sums up how much less I had connected with this group than the last one. I had given every teacher I knew from the previous group a goodbye hug. Even if they were all present, I probably would have only embraced like five or six of the group.

The night before Anthony left, the Tanzanian students we had met (Poppy and co.) all came around to say their goodbyes. I bid them farewell also as I would be leaving Changzhou on the same day. We all hung out in Anthony's room, listening to music and playing chess. I was in diabolical form, blaming fatigue for a string of poor moves, which allowed me to be beaten by someone who only learned how to play about a week ago. We spoke about racism in China. I was pleased to learn that Poppy's tolerance was even lower than mine was, saying he had even resorted to pushing or kicking out at people who crossed the line. I commended him, as I believe lessons of this nature are best learned the hard way, and I doubt anyone on the receiving end of his reactions would repeat their actions when they crossed paths with another Black person. In all honesty, I regretted not being more outwardly aggressive at certain times, but I could not shake the sense of caution from being in a new country.

Additionally, I was told early on that some Chinese locals are known to pick fights with foreigners. Chinese collectivism apparently means witnesses would always take the side of the local and conspire for the foreign party to receive the full brunt of the law. I was less willing to take that chance.

Anthony and I said our goodbyes, reminiscing on an eventful year. We had struck up a genuine friendship resulting in us both reassuring each other we would meet again. Poppy has a mother who lives in London he visits, so I also planned to see him again. I want to visit Tanzania one day to see his homeland as well, so potentially I would see everyone else I met out there.

On the last school day of the year, I went on an unofficial lap of honour where I briefly interrupted lessons to say my goodbyes. The friendlier teachers allowed class photos while others forced me to keep it brief so they could continue with their lessons. One or two teachers did not let me in at all. The fact I had barely taught my classes for about a month did make it feel a little anticlimactic. We had hardly seen each other, and then I popped in out of nowhere to say goodbye. At least there was some closure.

There was also the small matter of picking up my extended visa. Despite my contract stating I would be employed until July 10th my services were only required until mid-June. The problem was I'd booked my return ticket to London for July 12th whilst my visa ran out before that time. This meant I had to get a humanitarian visa, which was the nation's official way of saying they understand my predicament and would allow me to overstay my welcome. Daniel had handled the situation for me, but I had to collect the renewed visa in person, which became more of an inconvenience than it should have been. I left out in a t-shirt only to get caught in heavy rain on my way there. I arrived and found out upon arrival that the offices shut down for lunch and I had to return in 2 hours. I waited at the bus stop with my clothes soaked through while the man next to me did his utmost to summon the reserves of his phlegm and project it from his mouth. Once the bus came, I made my way towards the back seats while a group of three men found something humorous about my presence. I stuck a middle finger up and said 'f*** you!' hoping my hostility compensated for any language barrier. They seemed to be taken aback, but one of them kept turning back and sniggering. My tolerance was at an all-time low. I contemplated turning the altercation into a physical one, but it was my last day in the city, and I did not want to get arrested so close to the finish line. I found a middle ground between my urge for confrontation and reluctance to start a fight and decided on throwing a coin at him. He managed to swat it away, but it was enough to discourage him from turning around again. Mission accomplished.

I returned to collect my visa 2 hours later only to find out they did not have a crucial document I needed for travel. As I had lost my passport a few months ago, I needed an official document explaining why some stamps would be missing from my new one. I gave this document to Daniel when he said he would help me sort my new visa. I reiterated the importance of the form, and he said I would get it back, so I was not worried about it until now.

I went to drop my dorm keys back into the office and saw Cathy. She gave me a forced hello before carrying on her conversation. Considering this was the last time she was going to see me, I felt disrespected. The relations between the senior staff and me here had been strained due to their incompetence and my minimal tolerance of it. I knew in Chinese culture it was seen as rude to confront authority head-on or be directly critical of anyone. They tend to beat around the bush that I ran out of patience for it early on. I found it rude to be so consistently poor at giving me the necessary information needed for me to do my job or live in comfort. Either way, I was at least willing to pretend I was going to miss her and say one last goodbye. Her snubbing me rubbed me the wrong way, and for me was confirmation that towards the end, their abandon was as much to do with their dislike for me as their incompetence.

Literally from my first day to my last day at that school, I had one stressful situation after another, which stemmed from their lax administration. They messed up my visa to the point that they rushed against the clock to stop me being deported before I had taught a lesson for them. They were unsuccessful in honouring my contract, giving me no English lessons. I was not set up with the Mandarin lessons I was promised. I was not allowed to go home for Christmas despite having no classes to teach. They tried to underpay me for the Spring Festival, they took over three months to fix my shower but miraculously solved the issue as soon as they needed the spare room to accommodate another teacher. And on my very last day, I was deprived of the document I needed to get home! They could get stuffed!

I packed the last of my stuff and left Qingying Foreign Language School for the last time, with my cripplingly heavy suitcase and dense humidity teaming up to exhaust me rapidly. I checked my vibrating phone to see that Daniel had sent me a printable image of the document I needed to get home. I sighed with relief and continued my heavier breathing pattern after dragging my luggage out of the school gates. Luckily a cab pulled up right outside, and my girl flagged it down. The cab drove us away from Qinying Wujin Foreign Language School.

With every second, I was being taken that much further from the place where I became Teacher James, or to my distaste, Teacher Black. It then dawned on me that I had not been called Teacher Black for the last 3 or 4 months of my tenure in the school or any derogatory variation of the word by any of the children. My one-man crusade to eradicate the word from their vocabulary, whether they were taught by me or otherwise, was actually a success. I was so caught up in my actual job as well as other challenges that arose. I was focused on replacing my lost passport, grieving for my uncle and other more common challenges that living abroad brings to people of all colours. I failed to realise that I had stood my ground, heavily outnumbered, to eliminate casual racism from the habits of these children and I had actually won!

My relentless reprimanding throughout the school had paid off. I went through a few months where I was never too busy nor too drained to stop a kid in their tracks and firmly tell them to never use those offensive words again.

I then thought back to the class I had, where my star student had called me a black bear. It also escaped me at the time that their behaviour considerably improved after I confronted their attitude towards me. I just hoped that my message resonated with enough individuals in the class to leave a long-term impact on their perspective. Primary school children are impressionable at that age. Many adults reflect on the experiences they had with their teachers in primary school, revealing the profound effect it had left with them for the remainder of their lives.

As a teacher and as a Black person, it gives me an immense sense of pride to even think I may have affected a group of children in such a positive way. It could impact how they interact with Black people they meet in future. It could also have a ripple effect with other children, relatives and people they meet in future, should they show the same parodical mentality towards Black people that I may have coaxed out them.

In terms of change, one school in the most densely populated country in the world may feel like a drop in the ocean in the grand scheme of things, but it's better than nothing. I changed as much as I could in my proximity, and as human beings, whether our reach is one school, one class, or even one person, that's all we can do. Not everyone has a reach of millions of followers, fans or people who are willing to listen to them, but we all have a voice, and a responsibility to use it if we can change something for the better. That responsibility is amplified exponentially as a Teacher. It's safe to say my legacy as a Teacher in China stretches beyond English and P.E. lessons.

My employers wanted a smiley foreign mascot who would learn choreographed dances at their ceremonies. Instead, they got me doing my utmost to shift their students' attitudes away from being casually ignorant towards people who share my skin tone. I would like to say they got much more than what they bargained for, but the fact I failed to deliver on being the smiley dancing mascot, I think they got considerably less! I did not regret a thing. I was more than happy to give up being a foreign caricature for a more just cause. It is fine to not meet the expectations others have of you, if it means the expectations you have of yourself remain uncompromised.

Fin

I was back in Nanjing, a free man reflecting on my year as a teacher. I was leaving the easiest job I would ever have but also potentially the worst employers, so it was a double-edged sword. When I say the worst employers, I may sound a little harsh. I was extremely grateful for their hospitality. The times Cherry took Anthony and me out for dinner and drinks with her husband and his work colleagues sparing no expense. Cathy invited us to her relative's wedding as well as taking us out to dinner earlier in the year. Daniel helped me without complaint every time I asked while living in China. All of those moments were touching, and I will treasure those moments forever. However, when it came to dealing with the basic administrative needs of my job, it was a nightmare! I had some great memories of the place, but I also could not be happier I was done with it. The feeling was surreal. I was done. No classes or lesson plans. Nothing. I was back in holiday mode. I was once again a tourist with nothing to worry about but travel plans, my next meal and whether I'd get to watch any more Euro 2016 matches.

With the academic year ending and a fortnight left until my return flight, I was allowed to enjoy the remainder of my time in China as a full-time tourist. It felt great having no commitments or constraints, being able to let loose without worrying about straightening back up in a given time.

I spent just over a week in Nanjing with my girlfriend. We were initially meant to visit Hangzhou, but the weather forecasts told us the duration of our stay was going to be mostly rain and thunderstorms. We decided against paying to travel and stay in a city with worse weather than where we already were. It proved to be the right call as we saved money and had a great time. We re-visited the Presidential Palace, went to Xuanwu Lake, which had some of the most picturesque scenery I've ever witnessed. I felt like I was in the scene of a Studio Ghibli movie. Lotus flowers were in full bloom and surrounded by lily pads, with the lake being bordered by a variety of trees. I enjoyed being in a place where cameras were out, and nobody cared enough to take pictures of us. And for a good reason. This place was breathtaking.

We also visited a museum and art gallery in Daxingong, which gave us an insight into the town's architectural and cultural history.

Between our tourist activities, we just chilled out. Eating at our favourite restaurants, playing badminton, checking out a few of the bars we were already acquainted with and anything where we could enjoy the summer weather at a low cost.

We ended our last full day in the Jiangsu province in the most fitting way possible; going to watch Jiangsu Suning FC live at their home stadium. I was excited to see the standard of top-flight Chinese football as well as seeing Ramires play. He had transferred to Jiangsu from Chelsea in January, so I relished seeing an old favourite of mine in action. It was a surprisingly good game. The crowd made for a lively and passionate atmosphere. The stadium was probably at less than half capacity, but those in attendance knew how to have a good time and exuded passion for the game. One fan acted as a cheerleader/conductor, with his back to the football pitch orchestrating the chants as he jumped around screaming. The quality was rather impressive, and our local heroes were on the right end of a

4-3 scoreline, so there was plenty of action. Ramires also scored an excellent finish from 20 yards. The icing on the cake.

The morning after, we lugged our suitcases through Nanjing's metro line to reach the airport and flew to Xi'an. We were greeted instantly by much more pleasant weather. The sun was shining, and the air was not as humid. We spent our first day seeing the Bell Tower and the Drum Tower respectively as our hostel was close to them. We also visited the famous Muslim Quarter, which we found despite a poorly scaled map and awful directions. It hosted a lively food market, rich with great-tasting options such as some of the best lamb skewers I had tasted, their signature beef baps and biang noodles. We visited there every day. The Great Mosque was in the Muslim Quarter too, so we saw it.

I raised an eyebrow at the fact vendors were selling counterfeit products right outside it and were exploiting it by charging for entry. The conversation with the Muslim man I met in Suzhou on Christmas replayed in my head. The compromised moral compass he was concerned about was displayed in full effect here, and tarnishing his place of worship taboot. However, this was nothing new, and the tourist in me wanted to see it. A vendor outside tried to sell me fake silk. I thought I would waste her time by exercising my bartering skills for the sport. I managed to get her down to 1/5 of her asking price, which was good enough for me, so I walked away.

I think I was super conscious of the mosque's tarnished sanctity as it was the month of Ramadan. Trading in a place of worship was always frowned upon, let alone trading fraudulent goods and lying to people barefaced about the quality. The Mosque was beautiful. It had some of the historical principles of Islam displayed around the place as well as impressive greenery and architecture.

The next day saw us at the world-famous Terracotta Warriors. It was amazing to see something so historic and monumental to a culture I had spent a year immersing myself in. During my time in China, I learned of the widespread beliefs of the afterlife, which come to the forefront on their Tomb Sweeping Day. Traditionally, families burn spirit money and paper replicas of material items from cars to homes. They believe people still require those things in the afterlife.

Qin Shi Huang, the first emperor of China, believed he would need an army to protect him in his afterlife. The result of this being the sculpting of the terracotta army being buried with him after his demise. I found it rather touching how, despite the cultural genocide the nation suffered under Mao, they clung onto similar beliefs to a people who roamed the country in 209BC and beyond.

The highlight of the trip was the bike ride on the city wall. We rented a tandem bike and took it for a spin around the wall, spanning around a considerable part of Xi'an. We were also lucky enough to go at a time where the pollution levels were relatively low, meaning our views were smog-free and managed to take in some breath-taking views as opposed to being short of breath due to low-quality air. My legs were feeling the burn afterwards. We went to a nearby bar afterwards to refuel, where I had two cheeseburger meals and enjoyed discounted cocktails.

After our time in Xi'an came to an end, we jumped on an overnight sleeper train to Beijing. It was my first time on a sleeper train, so I was quite excited to add it to my list of experiences. It did not go without an eventful time in the train station, which surprisingly felt a lot more industrial and less modernised than any train station I had seen in China so far. I guess I was spoiled by futuristic-looking Metro lines and fancy bullet trains. I assumed the popularity of Xi'an among tourists and the general stature of the city would have followed with a revamped station.

I experienced their not so modern facilities first hand when my bowel movements attempted to ambush me, resulting in a sprint across the station into the toilets.

For the second time in my trip here, I got caught out by the fact they do not provide toilet paper in public toilets. Last time I had to use some pages out of my notebook. This time I had no choice but to sacrifice my boxers. I stepped out of the men's room going commando only to realise there was someone right outside selling toilet paper for next to nothing. I must have sprinted past him in my desperation. Ah, well. Good thing I was wearing a pair of cheap underwear.

I reunited with my girl back in the queue for our trains, and we waited. During this time we were approached by a teenage girl, looking no older than 14 and wearing braces. Her parents were behind her smiling goofily in anticipation as she struck up a conversation with us. I braced myself for another native ready to practice their English.

The conversation followed the usual script. Exchanging names and ages, us being asked where we were from, her being taken aback by me revealing I was born in England because I am Black, me explaining there are a lot of Black people in England. During this exchange, a bit of a crowd started gathering. A mundane conversation between a Chinese teen, a Black man and Indian woman, was something you would not bat an eyelid at in London, but here, it was somewhat of a spectacle.

What I found weird was when she started discussing our appearance. She turned towards my girl and said, 'He looks different. You look more like us.'

This struck a note with me as I realised a lot of people in the country must think like her. It was not just by the racial background she was judging people but more in comparison to their "Chineseness" or likeness to it. Because my girl had a lighter skin tone to me, she was seen as closer to Chineseness to me, which in their eyes was positive.

She then said to me that I was very black. Seeing as she was in a talkative mood, I thought I would take up the opportunity to explain to her how rude that statement was. She did not seem to care. Instead of listening to what I was telling her, she rigidly stuck to what appeared to be a premeditated script of questions. I kept trying to make my point while she kept speaking over me and firing more questions. I got the impression she couldn't care less about what I had to say unless it fit her narrative or served the purpose of what she hoped to gain from the conversation. This inevitably agitated me. A man emerged from the crowd and extended his hand, and the girl felt the need to translate to me that the man wanted to shake my hand. I began to feel like a circus monkey being asked to do tricks.

'I don't want to shake this guy's hand,' I muttered to my girl.

'Then don't,' she replied.

I declined to do so, which resulted in the girl shaking the man's hand as if she was giving me an example of what was expected of me, assuming I didn't understand. This 'circus monkey' vibe became even more justified. They believed I did not understand the request before concluding that I was refusing the handshake as an autonomous human being.

She then tried to continue speaking before I interrupted and said as clearly as I could, 'I don't want to talk to you anymore. You are rude, and I don't like you.'

This took her aback, but thankfully she heard my message loud and clear. She turned away, and the crowd slowly lost interest and reformed their queues. I discussed what had just happened with my girl, and we agreed on the conclusions I had highlighted in the notes above. Neither of us could wait to get back home where we would be considered normal again.

The sleeper train was pretty cosy. We stayed in a 4-bed cabin and roomed with another couple. The bed was surprisingly comfortable. We were in bunk beds, which was a nice throwback to my childhood. It also meant fairly minimal communication between myself and my girlfriend as we didn't want to disturb the other couple. Not that I was feeling suffocated, but after being side by side with someone non-stop for about a month, it's always a positive being able to have time to yourself. I was in the bunker with her and two others but being on the top bunk isolated me from everyone and gave me the feeling of being alone. I allowed my thoughts to wander before drifting into a slumber, while the train gently rocked its passengers until it reached the final destination of Beijing.

During our time in the Chinese capital, we visited the monumental Tiananmen Square and Forbidden City as well as the Temple of Heaven and Earth. I had not seen the Forbidden City on my first visit to Beijing as it was closed for ceremonial marching, so I was glad I had a second chance. The Summer Palace was particularly impressive as the weather was fitting to the location's name. We had a bit of time to relax and enjoy the scenery as opposed to seeing something, taking pictures and swiftly moving on.

We rounded off our adventure by spending our last day on the one and only Great Wall of China. It was my second time on the wall, but it made the views no less phenomenal. I also went on a different part that was more horizontal. Consequently, I got to admire the view of the actual wall rather than what I could see from the heights it took me to. We raced down from the wall on toboggans which was a lot of fun, despite being frustrated by a girl in front of us slowing us down and interrupting our desire to live a real-life Mario Kart moment in some fantastic scenery.

That was the last of our tourist festivities, as we had to prepare ourselves for the flight home. I was flying back to Gatwick, and my girl to Heathrow and our flights had about a 12-hour gap between them, so I was set to get a train to the airport in the evening while she stayed overnight and followed in my footsteps the next morning. We spent the rest of the day packing our suitcases, sorting documents and taking it easy in the hostel facilities until it was time for me to go. Once that time came, my girl came with me part of the way so she could keep me company and wave me off once I boarded the express train into Beijing International Airport.

Being so preoccupied with enjoying what Xi'an and Beijing had to offer meant that I never really had the opportunity to ponder the prospect of going home. But now I was alone. Seated in the airport terminal fiddling with my phone as I waited to be summoned to board my flight. I was going home. My family. My friends. What have I missed? How was everyone? What's changed? I was so excited to find out the answers to these questions. To walk around my local streets and feel like I belong again. To feel human. No weird stares or pointing. No opportunists sneaking photos of me. I would allow myself to feel relaxed entirely when venturing outside again. I could not wait to indulge in Mum's cooking. Curry goat. Oxtail. Jerk Chicken. The list goes on. Drink cider. Go to a chip shop. All of these things were an 18-hour connecting flight via Istanbul away.

I had come full circle in my journey. I began my China experience in Beijing, bright-eyed and bushy-tailed, excited for the steps I was yet to take on the path ahead of me. Now I was back in Beijing at the airport, awaiting my flight home. That same path had now had my footprints all over it. There was smooth terrain, mountains to climb, glorious highs and soul-wrenching lows, but I had made it. I had come out of the other side, with my head held high after taking all the punches this country had to throw at me. I stepped onto the plane with an unshakeable sense of accomplishment, ready to close the book on what was hands-down the most noteworthy chapter of my life thus far.

It left me with a story to tell, lifelong friends, decoration for my CV and also a pretty good idea for a book. The surreal feeling of my journey coming to an end descended onto me as the wheels of the plane raised from the tarmac as we prepared to greet the skies. This was it. I was coming home.

Post-China

How It Changed Me

I feel like my journey in China left me with an air of fearlessness. I felt, and still do feel like if you can throw me into the deep end of life as a Black-British immigrant in China and I can keep my head afloat, there was not much else life can throw at me that I cannot overcome in the long run. I feel like beforehand I had already had a level of self-belief beyond most people, but this experience emboldened me even further.

The events within my friendship group back home during my travels showed me that as long as I know I am staying true to myself, anyone that could not accept me was expendable. Anyone. No matter how close you may think you are. The friends in that group I maintained are proof that if true friendship is reciprocated, they will accept your growth as a person regardless. If any disagreements come to the forefront, both parties should be willing to put their pride aside, accept any potential wrong-doings and continue to move from strength to strength. With that more instilled into my belief system more than ever, the influence of my peers' opinions on my decisions was at an all-time low, and believe me, it was already pretty low. My life is my own, and I refuse to allow my thoughts and actions to be limited by the perspectives of anyone.

On the other hand, the changes caused by my journey weren't all positive, though. The hostility brought out of me by the levels of unwanted attention and racial abuse I suffered out there also came home with me. As a defence mechanism, I was always on edge, ready to deal with the expected behaviours I deemed unacceptable that came with the territory of being Black and being outside at the same time. I felt like every time I let my guard down something would happen. So I stopped letting my guard down. It was exhausting, but it felt necessary for me, especially towards the end of the trip, where I would be visiting a lot of tourist spots, and everyone was already in photographer mode. To them, I was another site on their travels, so many cameras turned in my direction, and a lot of phones were snatched from my hands because of it. When disagreements arose, my responses were more sharp, ruthless and heated than what those who knew and loved me expected.

These changes were highlighted by members of my family as well as my girlfriend. I did not realise what was happening with me until it was pointed out to me, and I was forced into self-reflection. You could say I was a little traumatised by some of my experiences, which was not surprising when you think about how long and how often I had been on the receiving end of unsavoury treatment. It dawned on me; I may not have handled it as well as I thought if I had allowed myself to become more aggressive towards the people I cared about most.

It wasn't something I struggled with once I realised. I just needed to become less instinctive with my reactions and tone down my verbal vigour in confrontations.

Reverse Culture Shock

There was a lot of talk about reverse culture shock in my preparations for China, and when I read blog posts from previous teachers. With that in the back of my mind, I braced myself for the impact of home discomforts taking me aback when I arrived. However, I did not experience any of it.

Besides jetlag, I settled right back into the swing of things. For example, when my friend Ade came to my house the day I landed, we both jumped around, screaming and hugging each other from the excitement of seeing each other. The next time I saw him, a few days later, we went back to the same old bro-hugs and pleasantries. Ade even said, 'it's the second time I've seen you in a year, but it feels like you've been here week-in week-out.' And I agreed. It felt so familiar. I felt that way with most things. Walking around the ends, being on buses, seeing other friends and family. The first time around felt surreal and euphoric, but the second time around, it felt so regular.

I did, however, have difficulties being back home. Of course, there was the initial elation of being reunited with everyone. I couldn't have been happier to see them. I'd missed so much in that year; my little brother's 16th, my little sister's 18th birthday, my Mum's milestone birthday (your age is safe with me, Mummy) and not to mention spending the majority of my Christmas alone. Just being in their presence had me feeling a sense of security that eluded me for a long time. I was home. The issue was I returned at a pretty hectic, stressful time, and everything felt a little disjointed. The house was being prepared for

343

renovations, and Mum was also unwell, awaiting surgery. This caused a bit of a disconnect as everything still felt surreal while the rest of the house was stressing about different things. There was also the fact that after living abroad for a year, you get pretty used to a certain level of autonomy that was starting to become compromised.

I was happy to help the household and pull my weight when necessary. That willingness would change when I was asked to delay my plans or errands to do a mountain of dishes when I had contributed to 0% of the used crockery. Small things like that which were the household norm that I had become increasingly disconnected with while living alone became agitating.

These were minute issues among much larger disagreements amongst us that were more personal and had a higher magnitude that I will not delve into. I will tell you that the result was I packed a suitcase and moved out. I went to Ade's house. He and his mother were kind enough to let me make the living room my own until further notice. I felt there was still an air of a 'my house my rules' mentality with my parents whenever it came to differing opinions which were intolerable.

I had just lived abroad for a year while fending for myself. I was not a wealthy kid traveller that had the luxury of exploring the whole of Asia with my parent's money. I worked and saved, scraped pennies together to fund the vast majority of my journey and paid my own way whilst out there. Not that I have anything against people using the resources available to maximise their life experiences, I am just saying it was not the cloth I was cut from. So I felt I had earned the right for my parents to relieve me of that approach as I proved I was not living at home because I could not survive without them, but because it was the best option for me. But if I felt I could not be happy at home, I would take my chances on Ade's sofa until I could land a post-China job and get on my feet.

A couple of weeks had passed, and I returned home to try and settle things after I had spoken to my Aunt and expressed my frustrations, and she translated them back to my Dad. The talk was a success, and I relieved Ade and his mother of the 6'4 burden taking up their living room and returned home. There have not been any problems since. They learned that if I cared enough, I was willing to live and die by my decisions regardless of who supported me. I also had the realisation I mentioned earlier about my hostility levels since my return and assured them I would regulate myself accordingly.

Work After Teaching

If I am honest, the year in China put me off of wanting to become a career teacher in the near future. I did enjoy the role of a teacher, especially with teenage children. This is a transitional age where kids are starting to define their characteristics and become their own. My personality also suits dealing with more matured characters, as my persona is on the calmer side of the spectrum. Although I can match the levels of animation and enthusiasm necessary to capture younger children's attention, I simply do not enjoy doing so. My demeanour manages to demand older children's respect without me having to raise my voice or use as many disciplinary tactics. I have the right balance of getting along with those age groups while asserting my authority.

However, it was not how I wanted to spend my life in the present moment. I felt like I had no right to go to classes and teach my students to maximise their potential and reach for the stars if I did not do so myself. I had dreams of my own I wanted to accomplish before I became a teacher and facilitated the dreams of others.

The stint in China did have the desired effect on my CV. It gave me something to help me stand out from other applicants and intrigued potential employers, filling them with questions about my experience. I landed an IT sales role in The City. It was far from my dream job either, but it seemed like a decent place to make a decent living while I decided what to do with my long-term future.

Unfortunately, circumstances arose in the workplace that forced me to deem it unsuitable for me to remain there. I would go deeper into what happened, but I am legally obligated to spare you the details. If this book sells well enough for the legal fees to become less damaging to my bank account, I might consider telling all one day.

I then shortly after landed another sales role in the sports advertising industry. We sold perimeter advertising at high profile sports matches/events. It seemed an ideal match for me in terms of the industry, but I was not a fan of the "Wolf of Wall Street" style of sales

I needed to adopt to be successful at it. My calmer demeanour became a disadvantage in this role, and I did not quite reach the necessary heights, so I switched to a research role.

I lasted around six months before one month I drew in grand total revenue of £0 and my employers thought it was best to let me go. I was planning on quitting the following month, as I did not enjoy it at all, so it had a minimal effect in terms of my plans. However, I had never been sacked before, so my pride did take a bit of a blow. I had also stuck the job out because I did not want to go back to my parents with the news I had quit another job. It could have easily given them the impression I was growing lazy under the comfort of their umbrella. Being sacked meant I could report back to my parents with the news and tell them my fate was out of my hands. They were reassuring when I told them, ensuring they knew if things didn't work out for me, they knew it would never be because of a lack of effort.

The demand for the hours necessary to succeed in the role was eating into the time I would usually be spending on my creative endeavours. Building up a client base in the early days of a sales job is easily amongst the most demanding tasks a working person could have. To do it right, you simply have to give your life to the task, and that was something I was not willing to do. For me, not having time to work on music or my writing is the most paralysing and depressing thought possible in terms of my existence. I tried balancing my creative ambition with a sales career and both always suffered.

If I was going to give my life to something, I wanted to make sure it was something I enjoyed, and that I was working towards a place where I would still be happy with 10 or 20 years down the line. I knew no sales role would give me that satisfaction. I decided not to pursue another office job I had no intention of keeping in the long run and work part-time while I work on finding a way to monetise my creative talents. The first step was finishing this book. I have several novel ideas I plan on working on afterwards, and I aim to become an author. I also want to write more articles for websites and newspapers, which I have done. However, I want to do so as a freelancer so I can write about subjects of my choice and switch my focus onto books whenever I deem it necessary.

I rap too, with my stage name being Taller Than Life. I had been writing lyrics as a hobby for about two years preceding my China trip and have continued doing so. I had recorded a few freestyles and gotten glowing reviews from my peers. I am also not alone in believing I'm more lyrically talented than the vast majority of rappers in the UK who have managed to make a living from themselves from the music industry. I am sure if I used the same work ethic I did building client bases for jobs I had no desire for, into honing a craft that means everything to me, opportunities will come knocking sooner or later. It is down to me to find a way to monetise the talents I have instead of wasting my efforts striving for jobs I don't even want.

Friends?

After my experience, I am a firm believer in absence making the heart grow fonder. I have met many new characters on my travels, and a number of them will remain good friends of mine. However, there is no replacing your every day ones. The friends I maintained a healthy relationship with during my time away were sorely missed, and it was euphoric being reunited with them. We grew closer. When convenience is taken out of the equation, it becomes more apparent who cares about you.

On my return to the UK, I have since seen the friends I had fallen out with. We have since spoken about what happened and put our differences aside, making amends while accepting we will probably never be as close as we once were. The necessary apologies were made and accepted. It is a mystery how they will react to my "Real Friends" part of this book, but I have said nothing I will not stand beside on discussion. I also feel like I have done a decent job in being vague enough with my explanation by discussing how I felt about specific scenarios without unearthing dirty laundry with the fine details. Either way. It's a bit too late to unpublish this book, isn't it?

Love Story

As for my girlfriend, we split up about a year after our return home. We began to grow apart, and our connection was not the same as it once was. We made a mutual decision to end things before our relationship began to get toxic, and we started to resent each other. It was a difficult conclusion to reach, but it was the right one. We had experienced a lifetime worth of treasured experiences during our three years together and have memories we will both hold dear. Despite this, we could not allow the shine of our memories, dupe us into thinking our future together would be just as bright. Cracks were beginning to show, and the people we were growing into seemed to signal that they were only going to enlarge with time.

There is still love between us in regards to an appreciation we have for the role we played in each other's growth and past happiness, but neither of us would have plans of trying to rekindle things ever again. We were no longer romantically compatible, and it's as simple as that. Last time I checked she had found love elsewhere. After a much-needed break from commitment, I have stumbled into a fruitful, loving and fulfilling relationship of my own.

We are on healthy terms as far as ex's go. We do not keep in frequent contact, but if I did call, she would answer the phone and vice versa. I still have a special place in my heart for her family too. They made me feel welcome and part of their family from the first time I visited. My fondness towards them will never fade.

I think we definitely will live happily ever after, but just not together.

Would I Return to China?

I have had many people ask whether or not I would return there to live, and my answer is never straightforward. For starters, even if I had the most wholly stress-free and euphoric experience there, it is an experience I have already lived now. There are so many other countries I could explore and experience. Some I may enjoy more, some less, but the world is a big place with endless sights, people and experiences waiting to be had.

To answer your question, I would live in China again, but I would not live in Changzhou. I enjoyed my time there and met some great people, but besides Wuxi, every city I visited in the country was better than Changzhou in every way. Places to eat, their treatment of foreigners, nightlife, scenery, tourist attractions, and even Metro stations that made travelling around the city much more manageable. In Changzhou, you were reliant on buses and cabs if you were not e-biking around. But like I said, the people I had met in Changzhou compensated for it all, so although I would go elsewhere if I were ever to return, I do not regret my choice of location one bit.

China is practically a sub-continent in itself. The cultures and climates change from province to province. If I was to return to China, I think it would be a waste to return to the same place.

In terms of living abroad, it will not be on my agenda anytime soon. Not because I do not want to or was put off by the experience, I just feel like I should set some foundations back home before I venture off again. I returned from China with no idea of how I wanted the next few years of my life to turn out or what I was going to do with myself.
I refuse to be in that position the next time I leave home for a prolonged time and return. I also want to be able to take advantage of any potential business opportunities that present themselves while abroad.

During my time there, I had a lot of ideas and saw a lot of potential for profit, but I lacked the capital to pull anything off. I also knew the year I was contracted for would equate to my time in China, so the time to strategize was not there. The next time I travel, I want to have more of a financial cushion to at least attempt to follow through on any opportunities I see arise and generally be less frugal in my lifestyle.

Until I reach that position, I do not see myself being too allured by any more opportunities abroad until I accomplish more on my own soil. I have books to write, music to make and I am not even close to achieving the feats I know I am capable of in either of these fields. I could, obviously, have a great time abroad, but deep down, I would feel like I was delaying myself from my long-term goals. I know people say you should travel while you are still young, but I am not going to uproot myself just for the sake of it. If the travel bug bites me again, then it bites me, but for now, I feel like the pursuit of my ambitions on home-soil is a fulfilling enough journey right now.

Verdict

The most accurate way to summarise that year would be to say it was the hardest, but still the best year of my life up to that point. I had the highest highs along with the lowest lows, and I would say the smiles definitely outweighed the frowns. Moving abroad, away from your close friends or family comes with its own unique set of challenges. Moving to China, a country with such different cultural implications, values, and social norms had somewhat of a multiplier effect, as the differences were so vast. It also became daunting when the literal distance from home crept to the forefront of your mind.

Obviously, the levels of racism negatively affected my experience and my opinions of China, however, I am glad I dared to venture into the unknown and explore it for myself. I feel like I have done a noble service by putting myself into the firing line so I can report the findings back to my curious peers. I would like to make it clear that I am not trying to tar the whole of China with the same brush. To begin with, my experience was a rather unique one, hence me writing a book about it. I have a number of Black friends who have nothing but great things to say about their experiences in China and some that are still in China who have forged great lives for themselves. I also met some amazing Chinese people. The man I met in Suzhou in the garden on Christmas was one of the kindest people I had come across. Jong-Ho took time out to teach me Kung-Fu as well as treating me to lunch a few times purely out of kindness. The teachers I worked with also displayed multiple feats of kindness despite falling short in other areas. The group of children I taught with Golnaz in the Summer Camp were the most special group of kids I have had the pleasure of taking under my wing. In all honesty, if the future of China rests in the hands of children like that, the country, as well as the world, will be in a much better place further down the line. We also have to remember that China, as a whole, is still extremely inexperienced with integrating with other cultures and people. A lot of what they know about Black people is what they are shown through Western media, who are setting an awful precedent when it comes to racial equality.

With that, China has an awful lot of work to do. If they have any interest in quelling this issue, I would advise them to import some experts on race relations the same way they have done for football coaching. They need external help and education on how bad their conduct is. Unfortunately, knowing the Chinese government's usual reactions to criticism, if this book rises to any kind of prominence, it will likely be banned from the country as well as its author.

I say that to say this: The whole experience, from the build-up and preparation for my journey to the reflection of it, had given me a new lease of life. When I applied for the role, I was struggling to find my feet in the world as a confused, uncertain graduate, stumbling my way through days. Now I am writing this more assured than ever in the person I am and want to become. There is no guaranteed success for me in any way, shape or form, but I know for sure I will not regret this chosen path as your heart only regrets the actions you do not take. The yearning of "what if's" haunting my existence will not be a problem as I found out for myself first-hand. The thought of leaving the familiar behind and venturing into the unknown can be an overwhelming one and seen as a risk you are not willing to take. So I'll leave you with this quote:

"Maybe sometimes it's riskier not to take a risk. Sometimes all you're guaranteeing is that things will stay the same." — **Danny Wallace, Yes Man**

Thanks for reading.

Printed in Great Britain
by Amazon

78175189R00205